GRIEVING DADS

To the Brink and Back

Kelly Farley with David DiCola

ISBN: 0985205180
ISBN-13: 9780985205188

Library of Congress Control Number: 2012935614
Grieving Dads LLC, Aurora, IL.

TABLE OF CONTENTS

AUTHOR'S PREFACE

If you have ever loved a child, then you understand what it's like to love someone more than you love life itself. If you have ever *lost* a child, then you understand more about hell than anyone could possibly be expected to know.

If you have lost a child, you also understand this isn't something you get over. Only those who have lost a child can understand the depths to which this pain travels.

Like most of the men who will read this book, I too am a grieving dad. I lost two beautiful babies over an eighteen-month period, and those losses have had major and irreversible impacts on my life. To be quite honest, my psychological response to these losses scared the hell out of me. I felt out of control — because I was out of control. I couldn't change the fact that my children died. I couldn't stop hurting. I didn't just cry — I physically wept inside. There were times when there were no tears, and it felt like I was convulsing internally.

All of this scary stuff started to pile up on me, and when I finally decided to check my "manly" inclinations at the door and seek a bit of help, I discovered that I was in for a surprise. Almost all of the resources I could find on the subject of grieving for a child was directed either toward women or "parents." I put "parents" in quotation marks, because in my experience, most of what I read for grieving parents was written for mothers. If I did come across something aimed at grieving dads, it was usually advice about how to comfort their wives.

I'm sure there's *something* worthwhile out there. But in the absence of anything that jumped out and kicked me in the head, I decided to pursue the issue myself. Part of the result can be found right here within these pages.

The message I want bereaved fathers to understand is that I know it's hard, I know it hurts, I know it's scary — but you can get through this. You can survive. It will be the hardest thing you will ever experience; it will drain you physically, mentally, and emotionally. You can come out on the other side of this very long and lonely tunnel, but you will be a different person when you do. There is no going back to the old you.

I also want all grieving dads to know that they are not alone in their grief. I want them to understand that other men have been through this and that the emotions they keep inside are the same emotions they'll hear about from the many men whose stories appear in this book.

Grieving Dads: To the Brink and Back aims to bring awareness to the impacts that child loss has upon fathers. It is also meant to let society know it's okay for a father to grieve the loss of a child. Society expects men to react differently than women. As a result, men oftentimes grieve in silence, usually when they are alone. A father shouldn't have to hide his pain or feel ashamed to show his emotions when dealing with the loss of a child.

I am also hopeful that this book will bring insight to the women in these men's lives about how their husbands, brothers, fathers, or male friends may be feeling.

You will hear from the men in this book that life has been forever changed after the death of a child. It is virtually impossible to continue through life as if nothing happened; you can't run from it, and you can't hide from it. Society expects men to "take it like a man," but it's not realistic or fair to ask a father to behave that way. The best thing any father can do for himself and for others around him is to reach out for help, and to know it is not a sign of "weakness" to do so. Instead, it's a sign of courage and strength — the kind that's required to face this battle head on.

During the deepest, darkest days of my grief, I made a promise to my daughter, Katie, my son, Noah, and myself that once I was strong enough, I would reach out to other dads that are traveling this lonely road known as unspeakable loss. I would do this to help these other dads come to terms with their loss, to help them find their way, to help them cope, and somehow, to help them survive this profound life event. I didn't know how I would do all of this, but I would find a way.

This book is a result of that promise.

DEDICATION

I dedicate this book to my beautiful Katie and sweet baby Noah. I deeply love and miss you both.

I also dedicate this book to my beautiful wife, Christine, who encouraged me and supported me throughout the creation of this book. Without her love and understanding I wouldn't have survived the death of Katie and Noah. She is one of the reasons I've been able to keep my promise and take steps along this journey to help other grieving dads.

CHAPTER 1

THE BRINK

THEIR STORIES ARE terrible.

All of them. The people in these stories are men who have been through the death of a child. Some of these men have abandoned any sense of what being a "man" may have once meant to them. Some are still trying to hold on to how society defines being a real man. Some of them abandoned God. Some of them *found* God. But all of them have held on to one thing that remains constant — one thing that never diminishes, no matter how much time has passed by.

To a man, they have held on to the overwhelming desire to trade places with their child. Willingly, and without hesitation.

I know I would have. So would they.

All of them.

The first of "all of them" was Angelo. Like me, he came to be a member of this horrible, not so exclusive club some years ago. Like me, to this day he continues to ask questions for which there are no answers.

But I asked him some of those questions anyway. And I did the same when I talked with Nick, Ed, Kent, Steven, and Phil, among many others you will get to know in this book. I did that, you see, because all of us have something in common.

We've been to the brink.

Some of us are still standing there, while others have started to back away from it.

For all of the bad things a man might encounter in his lifetime, there can be nothing that comes even close to the loss of his child.

According to Nick, "Losing a child is the *worst* loss a human can feel." This he says from a knowing perspective. The kind that comes from losing a daughter to a heroin overdose.

There were many other "knowing perspectives" gathered while talking with the grieving dads I've met. Like the one from Kent, who watched his son, Chris, take his last breath at the scene of a motor vehicle accident.

Or Ed's "knowing perspective." His came as a by-product of finding his 17-year-old son, Joey, hanging from a ceiling fan.

Ed helped cut Joey down.

And afterwards, like many fathers who have had to endure the shock, trauma, and agony of losing a child, Ed often wished that something would happen to him, not only because he wanted the pain to stop, but he wanted to see Joey again — if only for the chance to ask him, "Why?"

I told you their stories were terrible, didn't I?

Well, I wasn't kidding. Their stories are indeed terrible, and quite purposefully raw. There are no candy-coated messages to be found here. No empty talk about another angel in heaven or the death of a child being part of God's plan.

So, if you are holding this book in your hands with the expectation that you're going to read the same sort of "self help" drivel you can find everywhere else, you're in for a disappointment.

If this book ever gets made into a movie, I promise you it won't be a chick flick. It wasn't written from a woman's perspective. It wasn't written by a Ph.D. in psychology. It wasn't written by an Oprah Winfrey book-of-the-month club author, either.

Instead, it was written by men who are part of a brotherhood shaped out of unimaginable loss, unbearable grief, unrelenting despair — and all the things that come along for the ride. Seemingly harmless things like averted glances or thoughtless comments. Not so harmless things like ruined relationships, new addictions, and a sense of apathy that threatens to destroy the last fragments of meaning in a man's life.

Some people will read this book and say it's "the truth." Others who read it will say that it's "morbid" or "dark." Well, let me tell you something. There is nothing — *nothing* on this earth as dark as the death of a child! But allowing these grieving dads to express themselves through this book, however dark it may be at times, is the best way I know to bring everyone involved back to the light of day.

Yes, we've been to the brink. And many of us are still teetering there, perched just as precariously as you please, vacillating from moment to moment about whether to seek rescue or simply give up and jump over the edge.

Fathers, you see, aren't supposed to grieve the same way that mothers do. Society has placed certain demands on men that preclude them from dealing with loss or disappointment by wearing emotion on their sleeves or even talking about it openly. For sure, men aren't supposed to lose control. They are expected to toughen up, get back to work, take it like a man, and support their wives.

And if they must cry, by all means they should do so in private.

My own journey through these dark expectations began with the crippling anxiety that comes from losing not one, but two children. If I thought that the death of Katie, the cherished little girl that I would protect and love forever, would be the worst I'd have to deal with in my life, I stood corrected just 18 months later when my son, Noah, died, too.

After Noah's death, I could no longer hide behind the denial that sustained me through Katie's passing. In dealing with the loss of Katie, the luxury of plunging myself into my work and the needs of my wife insulated me from my own buried emotions, as I told myself above all else to simply keep *moving*. There was no time to stop and think about things or allow myself to feel anything. If a chink started to appear in my carefully constructed armor — if I began to "let my emotions get the best of me" — I just hit the gym or dove into a home improvement project.

And of course, I never, ever talked about how I felt.

But when we lost Noah, my body and my mind completely shut down. None of the things that helped me to reject the reality of losing a daughter would suffice in the wake of losing a second child. Forget the gym — I barely had the energy to get out of bed. Forget work, too. I saw no point in it, and couldn't have completed the most mundane tasks even if I could have made it to the office.

Forget everything.

For the first time in my life, I really didn't care if I lived or died. In fact, in the three months after Noah's death, the greatest effort I exerted was making a phone call to my office to take a leave of absence. I wasn't asking for permission, either. I was making an announcement, and if the job was still available should I decide to return — fine.

If not, I couldn't care less.

During the time I was away from work, I started a desperate search on the Internet, seeking other dads who had gone through the pain I was experiencing and who could maybe give me some reasonable insight into what I was going through.

For the most part, this was a waste of time. I found very little out there on the Web that came from other dads, and the few grief support resources I did encounter were aimed at moms instead. Sometimes, there was information available that was geared toward couples — but when they specifically mentioned the fathers, most often they gave advice about how husbands could help their wives through the tragedy.

In short, as a grieving dad looking for answers from other grieving dads, I was quite apparently shit out of luck.

That's pretty much why I wrote this book.

Like most men, when there is a problem, I am inclined to look for ways to solve it. The lack of support for grieving dads is a good example of a problem — one that could perhaps be fixed if there was some kind of resource out there for dads. Since I couldn't find such a resource when I needed it most, I set about creating one.

The result? This book, among other things.

Within these pages, you will meet several fathers who, like me, understand the depths to which this pain travels.

Yes, their stories are terrible. But as close as their stories came to pushing these men over the brink, they also helped to pull them back.

Read these stories — terrible as they may be. Because if you do, I promise they will shine some light on more than just one path back from the brink. And with a little hope, maybe you'll find one of those paths to be the direction you've been looking for all along.

CHAPTER 2

SHOCK & TRAUMA

IF IT WERE UP to me, I probably would change the "five stages of grief" thing so it included a brand new category. I'd call it "Shock and Trauma," because those are really the things that hit you first after the death of a child.

"Shock," minus the awe. And "trauma," minus the blood. Leastwise, trauma minus your *own* blood.

The experts call the first stage of grieving "denial," and I can promise you that you will indeed experience denial when you go through the loss of a child. You just won't get there without experiencing shock and trauma first. The kind of trauma that impacts your nervous system to a point that is irreparable. The crossing of a threshold that has lasting effects on your mind, complete with images and words that forever will be with you.

For a glimpse into what I'm talking about, consider the story of Nick.

Nick was making breakfast for his seven-year-old son one morning. His 17-year-old daughter, Michelle, should have been downstairs by now to join them for the day's first meal. Instead, Michelle was still in her room, lying dead from a heroin overdose, the wall beside her bed covered in vomit. Her face already a pale blue.

Nick's wife had been trying to get Michelle out of bed, but she wouldn't wake up. Little wonder. She was gone, a victim of a new epidemic sweeping the nation's teenage population. Michelle got caught up in this new heroin epidemic before the community even knew it was an issue. And lest you think that Michelle was a troubled child that had shown all sorts of "warning bells" related to the choices that led to her death, you should understand that Michelle was an honor roll student. The kind of kid that had so many friends, over 500 people showed up for her funeral.

To this day, Nick blames the person who gave Michelle the tainted drug. Finding Michelle asleep, forever, in her bed that fateful morning will forever haunt Nick. So will the fruitless attempts at CPR. The screams of his wife. The call to 911. The cop car showing up first, the ambulance after. All for nothing, because it was too late for anyone to help Nick's little girl by the time the sun rose on the day she died.

In a survey he filled out, Nick tells me, "You will never experience a pain like this."

Well, he's right. Like I said, shock and trauma.

Grief from the death of a child *is* trauma — a fact I simply didn't understand when I was a newly bereaved father. But time and time again, this wisdom proved true for me and for all the dads I interviewed. Some of us watched our children die slowly over weeks or months. Some of us were left reeling by a sudden, unexpected death. Some of us actually *witnessed* one of those sudden, unexpected deaths.

And some of us, like Kent, had to deal with the shock and trauma of losing more than one child.

For his first encounter with the death of a child, Kent lost his daughter, Sarah, just one day after she was born. A genetic disorder by the name of Trisomy 18 claimed Sarah, just as it does half of its victims in their first week of life. For the other 50 percent, survival into the teen years is possible, but perhaps not recommended. There are complications, most of them gruesome, and all of them caused by a glitch in the eighteenth human chromosome. Physical deformities, scarce mental function, and almost no shot at ever seeing the age of 20. All part of the wonderfulness of Trisomy 18.

These are things, unfortunately, that I am all too familiar with myself. Genetic disorders, I mean. My son, Noah, and my daughter, Katie, both followed Kent's precious Sarah down the path of hereditary dysfunction caused by genetic disorders. And Kent, unfortunately, followed me down the path of knowing the pain, shock, and trauma of losing more than one child.

Kent's second loss would come without the help of some rare genetic fluke, but rather through a not so rare accident involving the family car. Kent was driving the car, on a day that started out like so many others. His wife was up front with him, and the two children that came in the years following Sarah's death were seated in the back. All three of his passengers were asleep.

Kent's new nightmare would start with a familiar nuisance, one that he had previously checked out with local repair shops several times. The tire light was illuminated on the dashboard. But then, the tire light came on sporadically anyway, giving a false reading whenever the outside ambient temperatures were elevated — which was the case on this particular day. Nothing to worry about, the mechanics would say.

This time, though, there was plenty to worry about. A little while after the tire light came on, Kent heard a noise coming from the back of the car that reminded him of what it sounds like to drive on rough pavement. He remembers thinking that he'd just let his 14-year-old son, Chris, sleep for a few minutes more, because Kent would have to wake Chris to get him to help with whatever was causing the noise. When the sound didn't subside, Kent did what any experienced driver would do: slow the car and ease it over to the side of the road.

That decision, correct though it may have been, would wind up costing Chris his life.

It happened because a rear tire blew out. The tire's bead rolled over onto the rim, causing the car to spin 180 degrees. Kent lost control, and when the car finally came to rest, they had crashed into a ditch.

The wrong ditch, as luck would have it.

This particular ditch happened to have the only rock outcropping in sight along the hillside next to this particular stretch of the highway. Accordingly, the entire back portion of the car was crushed inward.

"Mom, Chris is bleeding!" were the first words Kent remembers hearing. They came from Claire, his daughter, who survived the crash but was the first to witness what it meant for her brother.

Kent scrambled to get out of the car and around to Chris's side, and what he saw next was seared into his memory forever. His son's head was crushed between the roof and the side of the car. The trauma was bad. The shock to Kent was, too.

His first reaction was to drop to his knees and pound the ground, screaming, "My son is dead!"

Within seconds, Kent's medical training kicked in and he went to Chris. There was still a pulse, and Chris was still breathing. But any hope that his son might somehow survive such a massive head injury would be gone in minutes. There was no response to the pain stimulus that Kent applied. And while Kent's hand was lying on his son's chest, Chris stopped breathing, and Kent felt the very last beat of his young son's heart.

Ironically, just hours before the tragic accident, the family had prayed together after coming across a traffic delay caused by someone else's tragic accident. They could not have known that soon they too would be the object of the prayers of strangers.

A doctor who happened by pronounced Chris dead at the scene. The coroner later estimated that Chris had died within three seconds of the impact; the breathing and pulse Kent felt afterwards were mere physiological responses of a body that no longer played host to Chris's vibrant young spirit.

The fact that Chris didn't suffer long was of little consolation to Kent, however. Chris and Kent were very close — Kent refers to the day Chris was born as the proudest day of his life — and throughout his son's short time here on earth, Kent did his best to include his boy in whatever activities he could. The two were practically inseparable during the boy's early years of childhood, and they had an exceptional relationship even into Chris's first year as a teenager.

Kent holds a conviction that one should never make someone out to be bigger and better in death than they were in life. Still, as he looks back, he can't seem to say enough good things about his son.

One of the questions I asked Kent was, "How has the loss of your child impacted your life?"

"How has it not?" was his reply.

In every conceivable way, the loss of a child alters your life and any plans you might have made for it. Kent is no exception; his plan for the future was to start an electrician's business with Chris. Of course, that part of Kent's plan evaporated at the moment he watched his son take his final breath of air.

As a bereaved father, Kent now has moments where he feels like he is afraid to live. This, too, I can relate with, as I've gone through so many similar emotions. I avoided grief for as long as possible after the initial shock wore off, of losing Katie and then Noah.

I've heard a saying about grief that goes, "You can close the door on grief, but it will peek in through the window." Although this saying paints an eerie image, I found a lot of truth in these words. I tried to ignore the pain I was feeling, but I learned the hard way that you cannot hide from this pain. It will find you and you will have to deal with it. Because even when the shock wears off, the trauma cannot be ignored.

Surely, there can be no trauma worse than losing more than one child, can there?

For an attempt at an answer to a horrible question like that, we might ask Phil. During my interview with Phil, who lost his 19-year-old son to a sudden death brought on by an enlarged heart, he made a comment I'll never forget:

> *"There isn't anything worse than the loss of a child, and if there is,*
> *I don't want to know about it."*

Me neither.

For additional perspective on the subject of "worse," we might also ask Ed, whose introduction to shock and trauma came when he received a call from his son, Shane, who told him that his brother, Joey (Ed's 15-year-old son) was "tearing up his room" in a fit of anger.

Ed is divorced from Joey's mother, who had custody of the boys. She was crying in the background when Shane phoned, and she had called the police in response to Joey's display of rage. Apparently, it was happening because Joey and his girlfriend had a fight, after which she elected to break off their relationship.

Ed told his son he was on the way to see if he could help calm the situation. When he arrived, the police were already inside his ex-wife's home, and they had taken up station outside Joey's door. They had not been able to get Joey to respond to their requests to open the bedroom door, which Joey had quite effectively barricaded shut.

Things were quiet inside Joey's room. Too quiet, as it turned out.

After repeated attempts yielded no reply from Joey, the police kicked the door in, revealing Ed's son dangling from the ceiling fan with the help of a makeshift noose crafted from a bed sheet. Ed and the police rushed in, and he held his son's body upward while the cops worked furiously to cut through Joey's sheet.

When Joey was free, Ed dropped him on the bed and ripped the home-made noose away from his son's neck. The police were able to get Joey's heart started again, and they rushed him to the hospital, but it was too late. Joey's brain had gone without oxygen for too long, so Ed and his ex-wife made the traumatic decision to remove life support a few days later.

All of this shock and trauma happened to Ed's family back in August of 2009. Today, Ed says that his life will never be the same. For a long time following the death of his son, Ed found himself wishing that something might happen to him, too. This way, not only would the pain stop, but he could also see Joey again in the afterlife that Ed firmly believes exists.

Priorities change for grieving fathers, and they changed for Ed, too. He was never very big on watching TV, but today he rarely turns it on at all. He finds more comfort in listening to music, especially the music his son's band put together before Joey died. One song in particular brings Ed closer to Joey — one that his son wrote and recorded on a CD that Ed still cherishes today.

Ed and Joey were artists, each in their own way, before Joey died. They both shared a love of music (especially bass guitar) and Ed has written three novels over the years. Now, Ed finds some additional solace in writing poetry, some of which he has shared with the Grieving Dads website. The following is one of my favorite thought-provoking passages from his poem "Why Did You Go Before Me?":

> *"Your music fills me still*
> *Yet now I'm strangely different*
> *than I ever was before*
> *Grounded and yet so willing*
> *to step beyond the door."*

Ed also finds some comfort in the knowledge that he has become a stronger person, and one who is willing to do what it takes to help save another life or ease another's pain. He doesn't believe in trying to hide from what happened, but he does believe in sharing his story wherever it might help.

Help, it seems, is what grieving dads need most, even if all they have been taught their whole lives is to "be strong" and "rise above the pain." But nothing that anyone could ever teach a man could possibly prepare him for the shock and trauma of losing a child.

Regardless of the circumstances surrounding the death of a child, the entire experience is terribly traumatic. The late night phone call. Holding your child when he or she dies. Having to make life and death decisions on their behalf. It's no wonder, then, that so many grieving dads suffer from post-traumatic stress disorder (PTSD).

The issue of PTSD as it relates to the plight of grieving dads brings to mind the case of Bryan. I interviewed Bryan just seven months after the death of his little boy, Charlie, who was a little over 2 years old when he passed away.

Bryan and I didn't discuss PTSD specifically during our talk, but the shock and trauma of Charlie's passing left Bryan in a state that clearly could merit such a diagnosis. He is no different from any grieving dad in that regard, brought on in no small part by the circumstances at hand when his son died of flu complications in 2011.

"It was the Monday — Martin Luther King Day," Bryan began, after I asked him to tell me what happened. "I had the day off. I suggested we go to the mall [with Bryan's sister and her son]. I let Charlie play on the jungle gym and afterwards we had lunch, during which my sister said, 'You know what, I didn't wash his hands.' The next day he came down with the flu and he had a fever into Tuesday night and then it was gone."

"Gone," as it would be proven later, was only a temporary thing.

Charlie seemed okay by Friday of the same week, so Bryan left for a preplanned trip to Las Vegas with several friends. By 4:00 a.m. Saturday, things took a big turn for the worse.

"My wife woke up to the sides of the bed rattling," Bryan tells me. "Charlie yelled out, 'Mommy,' and she went in there and he was having a seizure and that was it. He continued to have seizures and the ambulance took 40 minutes to get to the house."

When the EMTs finally arrived, they suggested that Charlie was stable. But Bryan's wife is a pediatric nurse, and she knew better. She insisted that her son be transported to a hospital immediately.

"We had just gotten back to the suite [in Vegas] when I got a phone call from my mom saying, 'Charlie's sick, you need to come home,'" Bryan continued. "So my friends helped me catch the next flight out of Vegas. My uncle was waiting for me at the airport when I arrived. When I got to the hospital, Charlie was having an MRI so I couldn't see him right away. Then they said they were going to bring him out to the intensive care unit, and that I should wait for him up there. So I waited up there for a little while but thought 'fuck that' and decided to stand by the elevator."

The instant the elevator doors opened, Bryan said he took one look at Charlie and knew immediately that the situation was very grave. "He was just gone," Bryan says. "His eyes were half open. His legs were sprawled out like a frog."

Bryan asked the doctor, "If he comes out of this, is he going to be…" referring to Charlie's potential future and his quality of life. The fluid generated by the flu attacked his brain, rather than the lungs as is more typical in such cases. The result was brain damage, a fact the doctor confirmed by saying, "probably," before Bryan could even finish asking the question.

All of the things leading up to Charlie's condition and the grim reality of his future were shock and trauma enough. But it would get worse, because the doctors indicated that Charlie's breathing and feeding would be facilitated by artificial life support. "Basically just a body kept alive by a machine," Bryan told me. "And to me, that's not living."

In the days that followed, Bryan spent a lot of time with his son. Each day, he felt Charlie's body grow a little colder. And each day, he and his wife came closer to the realization that taking Charlie off life support was the right thing to do.

At the funeral, Bryan stood by the casket for six hours. "Everyone kept asking me to sit down or go to the bathroom or get something to drink. After the third or fourth person said something, I looked at them and said, 'If another person asks me that I'm going to deck them.'"

In addition to the overwhelming shock and trauma of living through Charlie's passing, today Bryan struggles with guilt over the possibility that simply making his son wash his hands before he ate would have avoided the whole thing. Guilt over going to Las Vegas with his buddies. Guilt over the fact that his eulogy of Charlie at the funeral service led to a standing ovation by those in attendance. And most of all, guilt over the idea that his wife had to endure the shock and trauma of Charlie's rapid descent without her husband by her side.

"She had to go through that horrific morning alone. She's a nurse and she sees the regression from the vibrant kid Friday night all the way down to hearing there was a pediatric code blue in the ER. She knows what that means and she knew exactly why it was called. So she's got the trauma of all that. She'll wake up in the middle of the night with nightmares."

When Bryan and I wrapped up our interview, he left me with one last thought: "It just seems like I'm empty. You know that feeling you get when you leave the house, and you wonder if you left the oven on? It's kind of like that. I forgot my kid. That's what gets me the most."

The shock and trauma of laying a child to rest can make a man feel like that, for sure. In my own case, I was completely unprepared for the shock that grief poured over my nervous system. The effects were physical, mental, and emotional, especially in the early going.

After the loss of my son, Noah, for the first time in my life I lost control. In the weeks and months that followed Noah's death, I often found myself paralyzed in the grip of fear and worry. I was worried that someone else around me was going to die and I would have to relive all of this pain. I worried about losing my job and spiraling out of control. I actually started to think that we were going to have to move in with parents or siblings so they could take care of us. I really wasn't sure if we would be productive members of society again.

I was feeling like this for no reason that my broken state of mind could fathom. Worse, when I wasn't afraid, I found myself horribly depressed, which was yet another state of mind I thought I would never experience, having wrongly been conditioned to believe that depression was for weak people and that it could be simply fought off with sufficient willpower. And even when I wasn't in a state of extreme emotional distress, I found myself flat on my back, suffering from exhaustion. It took almost everything I had to get out of the house and go to work. The first year I really didn't do a whole lot while I was at work; I would drive home thinking, "What did I do today?" Looking back, I can honestly answer that with, "Not much."

No desire to eat. No desire to move. In fact, I could barely drag myself out of bed — but more to the point, I didn't want to. For the first time in my life, I honestly didn't care if I lived or died.

These are the kinds of emotions that most grieving dads have described as "common" during my discussions with them. If you or someone you know is feeling them now, it's important to understand that **you are not alone**. These emotions are, in simple terms, part of the collateral damage the shock and trauma of a child's death inevitably brings.

So, what is a grieving father to do? How does he "pick up the pieces," so to speak, and find a way to power through all this shock and trauma to allow himself to grieve in some kind of therapeutic way?

For me, picking up the pieces started out one second at a time and gradually progressed to one minute at a time. The biggest thing is to find something to cling to — and whatever it is, do not let it go. Do whatever it takes to survive. Find a counselor or someone outside of the situation to speak with about what you are feeling. Someone who will listen without trying to solve your problem, because this problem cannot be solved — it can only be processed. It's important to start the processing, as difficult as it will be, as soon as possible. It is important to ask for help, and it's important to recognize that *asking for help is not a sign of weakness!*

It is a sign of courage instead.

As stated by R. Allan, whose 17-year-old son was killed when a vehicle struck the bicycle he was on, "There is no formula for this. Each person, each circumstance, each need is different. I say we know the unknowable."

And along with the observations of the grieving dads I've mentioned here, I have an important one of my own. The most crucial thing I learned about the early days of my own grief is that I had to actually experience the shock and trauma before I could ever possibly hope to get past it. My physical and emotional collapse had all the symptoms of PTSD, *which was a perfectly natural response to the trauma I had endured.* You see, my mind and body were screaming at me to stop and acknowledge what had happened, instead of continuing to push it away in some ridiculous attempt to ignore it.

In other words, I had to experience grief so acute as to be deemed nothing short of trauma — which of course, was the very thing I was trying to avoid.

What I know now is that the shock and trauma cannot be avoided. It must be recognized, and yes, even embraced. Until a grieving dad will take the time to truly feel the trauma he's been exposed to, he will never be able to understand the damage that has been dealt to him — and worse yet, he will never find the path that leads away from the brink and back toward the hope of a life full of meaning and purpose.

CHAPTER 3

SOCIETY'S EXPECTATIONS

CONVENTIONAL WISDOM AND its ideal grieving man is a carica-
ture. He's a stoic, John Wayne type who ruggedly weathers adversity and
climbs back in the saddle. Or, he's a battle-scarred fighter who silently
absorbs blow after blow, yet never hesitates to drag himself up and face his
opponent every time he's knocked down to the canvas.

The truth, however, is that no man can really live up to such standards.

"Dads are supposed to just be strong and move forward," says Leonard,
whose daughter was taken from him in a cowardly act of violence.

Murder, to be more precise.

Leonard's comment echoes those of many grieving dads, the wild majority of whom agree that society simply does not allow fathers enough time
to grieve. This phenomenon was uncovered through the questionnaire I
designed for this book, which posed a deceptively simple question:

"Do you feel society gives men enough time to grieve?"

Just as I'd suspected, this short question opened the door to an abun-
dance of opinions and observations on societal expectations surrounding

men's grief. This is a complex topic worthy of many books, and it's not possible to examine all of the issues and implications in a single chapter. Rather, my aim here is to present a general portrait of the experiences of the grieving dads who responded to the survey. I also hope to make a few observations that any grieving dad can benefit from, as a result of examining these common and hauntingly familiar experiences.

Though based on a small section of the estimated half-million U.S. fathers who lose a child every year, of all the grieving dads I heard from, only two of them indicated that they were given ample grieving time. I'm willing to bet that the sentiments reflected here will ring true for many readers, male and female alike. And it's little wonder, given the traditional views society seems to have when it comes to how men are supposed to carry themselves in the face of adversity.

"Society in general has no concept of the depth of pain a grieving father experiences," writes Jon. His first son died just one second short of making it to 13 hours of living, breathing life here on earth. Jon and his wife also experienced the loss of two additional children through miscarriages.

Now, after all of that, Jon is very sensitive to what grieving parents go through. If only he could say the same for the rest of society.

We'll visit with Jon again later in the book. For now, Jon believes (as I do) that society expects a grieving dad to be the stronger of the two parents. To be blunt, many fathers feel that they are really not allowed to grieve at all. And if there is some allowance for grieving, it seems to be universally expected to occur over a finite period of time, after which we grieving dads are supposed to simply "get over it" and move along with our lives.

Need some more evidence?

How about the comments of Kent? We met Kent back in chapter two, where we learned about his son, Chris, and how he passed away after a car accident during which Kent was driving. According to Kent, most people "have no idea and kindly dismiss [my grief] like it should be done by now."

Or, we could look to Matt, whose friends and associates were telling him it was time to move on and to be stronger, just a month after Matt lost his daughter.

A month? Really?

Another grieving dad, Ernie, reported that eight months after his daughter, Mel, passed away, his boss pulled him aside to tell him he was concerned about his performance. "You don't seem like yourself," the boss said.

Believe it or not, the boss then followed up with:

"It's like you're distracted or something."

When Ernie confessed that he was having difficulty dealing with the death of Mel, his boss was perplexed. "But it's been eight months," he said. "Shouldn't the grieving process be over with by now?"

The experiences of Ernie, as well as those of Leonard, Jon, Kent, and Matt are bad enough, for sure. Just hearing about these kinds of experiences irritates me and confirms that bringing awareness to the unique needs of grieving dads is essential. But worse, such experiences are rarely limited to comments made by bosses, co-workers, friends, or society at large. Sometimes, these unrealistic expectations are promoted by the closest family members of grieving dads.

In one particular case, Ed, reported that mere months after the death of his son, Jesse, he was admonished by his father-in-law — someone that had lost a son himself, no less — for keeping photos of Jesse around his house. "You need to get rid of this shit," his father-in-law said.

For an even more compelling example, consider the case of Cherie and her experience with her ex-husband, Mike. Cherie and Mike had gone through the loss of two daughters within a two-year period. Their second loss was their little girl, Robin; she passed away in her crib as a victim of SIDS.

Upon the horrible news of losing a second daughter, Cherie and Mike flew from Texas, where they were living at the time, back to New England to be home with their family. Mike hadn't uttered a single word since they found their daughter just hours earlier. When they landed and Mike saw his father at the airport, Mike finally let go of all he was holding inside and at last, he broke down and began to weep uncontrollably.

Cherie, for her part, was relieved. She knew that Mike was hurting himself by keeping the shock and trauma internalized, so she was glad to see him releasing it.

Mike's father, however, had different ideas. Instead of grabbing Mike in a consoling bear hug, Mike's father put both hands on his son's shoulders and said:

> *"Now stop that. Pull yourself together*
> *and act like the man I raised you to be."*

Well, Mike did exactly as his dad suggested, and Cherie never saw him cry again. Instead, Mike found solace in alcohol, and like many grieving parents, Cherie and Mike eventually wound up getting divorced.

Mike's experiences as a grieving dad are all too common, and they help to reveal that society's expectations are molded and imposed in different ways — but often with similar results. In Mike's case, his very own father impressed upon him society's rules about how men are "supposed" to act. By telling Mike to behave like the man his father had raised him to be, Mike was effectively ordered to put aside his emotions and ignore his natural (and necessary) longing to grieve.

In defense of Mike's father and his actions, he no doubt came to his conclusions about the "right" way for a grieving dad to carry himself through exposure to society's ideals regarding "manliness" in today's world. That exposure led to Mike's father giving the only advice he knew how to give, which was the equivalent of, "man up," as it were.

Man up. Stop that. Get over it. Be strong. Don't cry. But if you *must* cry, by all means, do so in private.

These are the things that mark society's expectations of men who are grieving over the loss of a child. And to me, they represent a very ugly version of "tough love."

For another perspective about tough love, we turn now to the story of Rich and his son, Jesse.

Jesse was a brilliant boy, but as Rich stated, "He had profound behavioral issues." By the time he was ten years old, Jesse had an alcohol problem. He'd do just about anything to acquire a buzz, including drinking mouthwash. In addition to using alcohol, Jesse caught on to the phenomenon of "huffing," which refers to the practice of purposefully inhaling various vapors in order to get a cheap high. Over time, Rich and his now ex-wife had to get rid of everything from cooking spray and cleaning fluids to nail polish remover and hair spray. Prescription drugs, of course, had to be locked away or kept off-premises, as well.

According to Rich, Jesse was, for whatever reasons, a very angry child. He could also be very sweet, but Jesse would sometimes become terribly vindictive whenever he perceived that someone was hurting him. As a possible explanation, Rich points to self-esteem problems that Jesse carried from the time he was a young boy. Rich also identifies family history as a source of Jesse's problems, which includes the deaths of Rich's brother and several cousins, all at young ages.

Indeed, Rich saw a piece of this dark family history in Jesse when he was just six years old. Somehow, Rich knew that Jesse would die before his time — he was so confident of this, that Rich told his older son:

"We will bury your little brother some day."

Rich did that to prepare his older son for his little brother's inevitable passing. In reality, Rich saw the writing on the wall, and he was doing what he could to get himself and his family ready for Jesse's death — including the preplanning of his youngest son's funeral.

Another form of tough love, it would seem.

Eventually, tough love became the only real approach Rich could conceive of in his attempts to turn around Jesse's life. In response to his son's self-destructive behaviors, Rich tried the tough love thing over and over. He dropped Jesse off at homeless shelters, just to give his son some perspective about real adversity. He signed Jesse up for a "scared straight" sort of boot camp, which involved two "drill sergeants" waking Jesse in the middle of the night and subsequently carting him off to Oregon. He even tried kicking Jesse out of the house, forcing his son to sleep outside in local parks with nothing more than a jacket for shelter.

None of it worked, really.

Jesse did become a bit less angry as he grew older, and in 2007 when he was 18, he had a brief period of sobriety. During this time, Rich thought, "I will enjoy him while I have him." He and Jesse became close during Jesse's interlude with sobriety, spending a lot of time together and having great talks on Rich's back porch. As this continued, father and son developed a very loving relationship.

But that didn't work, either.

Before long, Jesse slipped right back into his drug habit. And finally, after spending what seemed like another good day with Jesse, Rich dropped him at the train station later in the evening. It would be the last time Rich would see Jesse alive, because his son died of a heroin overdose that very night.

Jesse's funeral, being prearranged as it was, would involve cremation. The service was to begin at 3:00 p.m. on the chosen day. And on that day, Rich would work until 1:00 p.m., because burying himself in his job would be the one form of tough love he was sure to find effective.

In my interview with Rich, he tells me that he feels he got some sympathy after Jesse's passing. He did not receive much empathy, however. He also feels that society is quite generous with its compassion toward grieving mothers, but that for a grieving dad, there is "nothing to assist a man in a male form of grief."

I hear you, Rich.

I can personally attest to Rich's observations in that regard. In the months immediately following the deaths of both Katie and Noah, I lost count of the number of times someone would say, "How is your wife doing?"

This is a kind sentiment, for sure. But the people delivering these tidings almost never acknowledged *my* pain.

Sometimes, that pain would subside just enough for me to think a little more clearly, and I'd use whatever energy I could muster to throw myself into some Internet research to find out if what I was feeling as a grieving dad was *normal*. I'd look for anything I could find about other dads who experienced what I had, who had firsthand knowledge of the shock and trauma I experienced. Maybe, I reasoned, if I found such a resource, I could finally develop some kind of clue about what was happening to me.

Unfortunately, I found very little that was directly from other dads in similar circumstances. As I mentioned before, most of what I encountered in the way of grief support resources was aimed more at mothers than fathers.

Understandable, I guess. After all, big boys don't cry.

For men, there is an underlying bias, sometimes spoken and sometimes not, that crying is a sign of weakness. We are supposed to be able to "rise above" expressing or even acknowledging the concept of sadness to the point that we'd actually dare to weep. Our own tears and the tears of other men embarrass us.

Why is this the case? Why is such a normal, obvious, and even *logical* human response to loss — loss of the most devastating kind — discouraged or deemed unworthy?

I submit it's because the way men respond to loss stems all the way back to the way most of us were raised as boys. What were we taught when we experienced disappointment, loss, or pain?

Shake it off. Rub some dirt on it. Quit your whining. Toughen up.

Then, later in life when we grew from boys into men, we were given the "grown-up" version of this insightful message.

Stay strong. Stay busy. Get back to work. Don't let your emotions get the best of you (like that's even an option). Don't think about it.

Take it like a man.

Perhaps that kind of thinking is the reason why grieving dads such as Rich and me have found out the hard way that we only hurt ourselves by not allowing any real time to grieve. For one grieving dad, this kind of thinking has him staying at work until the last possible minute before he must leave to attend his son's funeral. For another, the desire to live up to society's expectations about supporting his grieving wife has him completely ignoring his own emotions.

And for all of us, society's views about what it means to be a man have had us feeling like we failed in our most basic of responsibilities — that being the role of the "protector."

Most fathers, if they are anything at all like me, have felt a strong conviction that protecting his children is perhaps his most important mission in life. We feel this way not only because of society's expectations that a father is to be the chief "provider" of the family, but also because we oblige ourselves to play the role of "protector" on a very basic and primitive level.

For a better illustration of how men become shackled by a sense of failure when they evolve from "protector" to "grieving dad," we can have a look at the experiences of Michael.

Michael lost his 3½-year-old daughter, Sylvie, in 2009. "Sylvie was the most amazing person I've ever known," Michael wrote. "She successfully beat — yes, I said beat — stage IV hepatoblastoma."

Hepatoblastoma is a serious liver disease that affects just one out of every 1.5 million children in the earliest years of life. In Sylvie's case, it started with what Michael and his wife thought was a routine stomach-ache. When it wouldn't go away, they took Sylvie to the doctor and she was diagnosed with cancer on February 9, 2009. Even today, Michael is still astonished at the disease's rapid progress.

"A tummy-ache became metastatic, stage IV cancer! After that, six months of pure hell. Six rounds of chemo, major liver resection, gall bladder removal, 120 days in the hospital, no eating or walking for six months... and I didn't know there was worse to come." Against all odds, Sylvie made a remarkable recovery. "She lost a negligible amount of hearing as is common with many pediatric cancer patients," Michael wrote, "but even that couldn't slow her down. She embraced her 'magic hearing buttons' as it was clear they helped her hear a bit better. She returned to school in September, somehow walking and sporting a crew cut."

Sylvie went back to her normal little girl activities of swimming, gymnastics, play dates, and all the other stuff little girls her age get to do when things are as they should be. Michael took his family to Florida the first week of November that year, and it seemed like the most triumphant time of their lives.

But triumph was to be a short-lived emotion, because just three months after Sylvie's miraculous recovery, the unthinkable happened. Michael once again found himself in an all too familiar setting — a hospital room, sitting next to the bed where his daughter was lying.

"We still aren't exactly sure why. Pneumonia? H1N1? Both?"

Whatever the reason, Sylvie died on November 29, 2009 — in a cruel twist of happenstance, the exact day of Michael's 40th birthday.

"Sylvie was snatched from us," Michael wrote. "All we have now are questions. And sorrow. And the feeling that I somehow let her down that day in the hospital."

Michael pointed out that society's expectations of men did indeed feed the guilt he experienced after Sylvie died. This feeling wasn't limited to the day of Sylvie's passing, either. In fact, it started way back when the news of her disease was first delivered.

"I did beat myself up when Sylvie was diagnosed," Michael wrote. "Hard."

As most grieving dads would no doubt have to agree, carrying the weight of losing a child is heavy enough. Pile on a few thousand more pounds of things such as guilt and a sense of "failure" at the very things we are most responsible for, and the load becomes unbearable.

For my own part, there were several times during the writing of this book that I wondered how I could go on. Narrating Sylvie's story was one of those times. To think that your child has beaten the odds, to get *so close to victory,* only to have your child snatched away from you as Michael so aptly put it, is simply more than any human could possibly be expected to handle.

But in another example of Michael's ability to boil things down in a pertinent way, he wrote, "I hope these stories get to people like me and in some small way, they help those of us who have to do the unspeakable and bury a child."

Well, that settled it quickly. If Michael could look at things in such a way, I certainly could. And it didn't take long to figure out how right he is about this. Michael, like all the fathers who participated in this book, courageously shared his own suffering in the hope of helping others.

To be sure, the brotherhood of grieving dads has kept me going, and I'd like to think it's helped Michael, too. In his case, even with the additional burden of what society asks of men who are grieving after the loss of a child, Michael has found a few effective countermeasures to help in easing the pain.

Looking back to the day Sylvie died, Michael remembers his daughter's last magic trick. At one point, Sylvie resumed breathing when it seemed most unlikely, and she looked Michael straight in the eye. "I realize that was her way of saying goodbye," Michael says. "For now."

Over time, Michael has come to realize that he did all he could to protect his cherished little girl. "If I am thankful for anything," he says, "it is that we were unequivocally perfect in regards to medical care before Sylvie passed away. I might be unable to deal with this at all if I felt I could have done more that day. I know I couldn't have."

Going back further into Sylvie's battle against her disease, Michael reflected upon how he was right there with her, fighting at her side. "I spent many nights sleeping adjacent to her at home and monitoring her home care — needles and IVs and heparain shots we learned to administer at home. I convinced myself that if I put the extra effort in she would be okay."

Then, when Sylvie found herself in trouble once again after her brief success at beating her long odds, Michael remembered his reaction when her vital signs crashed. "In the hospital, I *ran* to get her assistance when her heart stopped, as the morons didn't have Sylvie, who had beaten stage IV cancer, centrally monitored. What if I had gone for coffee?"

But Michael didn't go for coffee. He fought for his little girl until the very end, and she knows her daddy did his very best.

In another of his philosophically adept moments, Michael says, "Grief, to me, is like a great chameleon. It hides in corners and changes shape, but in the end it always returns to its proper form — sadness, isolation, hopelessness, unfairness, bitterness, and all those other feelings that crowd my mind."

And when it comes to men, it's pointless to even "go there" in exploration of all those feelings. "Everyone knows [the loss of Sylvie] is the 300-pound beast at the bar, but no one has the balls to 'man up' and even ask, 'Hey man, how are you?'"

In other words, they already know the answer to that question, so why bother asking? Besides, given this whole concept of "society's expectations," Michael submits that most of his friends think he should have "moved on by now."

For Michael, the pain of losing Sylvie was still present, even as the one-year anniversary of her death approached. "That helpless feeling that started the day she passed has not left me," he explained. "No amount of therapy, drugs, or otherwise seems to help. It feels like I'm in an epic battle not unlike PTSD."

Yet life goes on. This is something that many grieving dads — including me — often have a very difficult time accepting. How can it be that life — work, social engagements, holidays, vacations, other people's joys and losses — continues to happen after our children die? How could any of those things *possibly* matter anymore?

Of course, those things do matter. Michael knows that, and to him, it matters that Sylvie did more than just "fight the good fight." She actually won.

"The one small thing I hold on to is that she *did* get better," Michael expresses. "She *did* beat stage IV cancer. We had an amazing three months that were probably the greatest imaginable, and never did we take a moment of it for granted. When we made our last trip to our mountain cabin in October of 2009, it was amazing how much Sylvie had come to love it. I can still remember her on my back in the hiker, her sweet weight, how she loved wild blackberries, how she played in the meadow. Her beautiful face."

Michael considers himself fortunate to have such wonderful memories. He also feels privileged to own his own business, and thus, he is not beholden to a supervisor's idea of when he should be "done" grieving — or how he chooses to grieve, for that matter. His business has been doing well, "so even though I'm certainly not all there," Michael adds, "I can skate by at my own pace."

He is indeed very lucky in this regard. He is lucky in other regards, too — especially given the fact that he became the father of twin boys in October of 2010.

Looking back over the experience of watching his wife progress through the pregnancy brings bittersweet thoughts to mind for Michael. There was excitement at the prospect of the twins' arrival. But there was also guilt over feeling such excitement.

For his new arrivals, the loss of an older sibling presents an all-new set of complications and anxieties, and at the very least, steals some of the shine from what should be 100 percent a joyful event. But now that his twins are here, Michael has high hopes that having Sylvie's little brothers running around will show him and his wife little bits of their big sister.

There was a time when I had such hopes, too. For Christine and me, Noah was to be our little reminder of everything we ever wanted for Katie. But when we lost Noah just eighteen months after Katie died, new grief compounded with old grief. Not only did I realize that those hopes were dashed, I also realized I wasn't going to live if I continued on my current path.

You see, at the time of Katie's death I was completely unaware that I was a textbook case of a father trying to meet society's impossible expectations regarding grief. I didn't know that I had absorbed all this "conventional" wisdom and that I was unconsciously following its dubious prescriptions.

27

All I knew was that I was experiencing a pain like none I'd ever felt and I wanted to make it stop. I also knew that my wife was living in that same hell, and I wanted to help her more than anything else.

Supporting a spouse or partner through grief is a wonderful and noble pursuit, but it can't come at the expense of your own mourning. Like many fathers, I sincerely wanted to help my wife, but I didn't realize until much later that supporting Christine became something like a "project" that I wanted to accomplish.

More to the point, I wanted to *excel* at this particular project. It was important to me to be *good* at consoling my wife. What I was missing in that equation, however, was that trying to "solve" Christine's grief was really little more than a wasted attempt at avoiding my own pain.

So many of the things I did — renovating the basement, the extra work hours, the fanatical workout routine — were ways of avoiding the hard work of facing and living through the difficult business of grief. I thought I was doing all the right things. I thought I was "taking it like a man" and "staying strong" and being "courageous" by suppressing my emotions. When the first sign of emotion began to appear — if I broke down sobbing or I experienced an anxiety attack — I fought it with all I had and chastised myself for being weak. I wanted to do battle with these unfamiliar and unwelcome experiences, and I wanted to win. I was determined to be a good soldier.

Bound and determined or not, before long I was physically, mentally, and emotionally exhausted. I had no reserves left to fight this ugly new enemy of mine.

Grief.

But once I realized that, once I came to the conclusion that I was out of weapons, I learned something. Something really, really important. I learned that grief is really not my enemy at all. Instead, grief and any way it might be expressed — whether through tears, anger, fear, physical exhaustion, illness, or a lack of confidence — is a *natural* reaction to catastrophic loss.

If there's any "right" way to grieve, if there's any "should" here at all, it's that we *should* feel extreme sadness, frustration, and anger.

And believe it or not, *we should feel pain.*

This may be obvious to some, but for me it was a necessary lesson. I'm reasonably sure there are many other guys out there who are as confounded

28

by their reaction to loss as I was, and thus had plenty of lessons to learn as well. Hard lessons, for sure. But very necessary ones.

Perhaps the most necessary ones are that I now know it takes *far* more courage to live through the pain of grief than it does to deny your natural reactions and emotions. And it takes *far* more courage to challenge conventional wisdom about how men should grieve.

Even more courage is required to give ourselves permission to weep, to take all the time we need to mourn, and to express our grief in whatever form we may need.

And as for strength? There is a time and place to be strong in the traditional sense of that word. Dealing with the death of a child is not one of those times. Because no man, no matter how tough he thinks he may be, and no matter how much the world expects him to be that way — is man enough to ignore the trauma of losing a child.

Not even John Wayne.

CHAPTER 4

STRAINED RESPONSES

EVEN FOR THOSE who aren't directly affected by the passing of a child, the cold reach of grief is as expansive as the crushing despair it causes. No one is exempt from the fallout — least of all the family, friends, co-workers, and the rest of the people that make up the community surrounding every grieving dad.

For sure, the death of a child that affects any member of a person's community will, in reality, affect *every* member of that person's community. Like many fathers who have experienced the death of a child, I have continuously found myself astounded by the strained responses that I have encountered since Katie and Noah passed away.

Those responses and reactions have not only been "strained," but they have also landed upon every conceivable point on the spectrum of possibilities. Some of the people in our community have tried their best to say something helpful, only to blurt out something insensitive or even downright insulting. Some have said and done everything right.

But others in our community have adopted perhaps the most strained response of all. They've distanced themselves from me, as if I am tainted in some way. Their reasoning? Perhaps they are afraid that if they draw too close, they will catch my "disease."

This kind of strained response is not unique to my situation. Over the course of the interviews I've conducted, the overwhelming majority of fathers have described similar experiences regarding the responses of the communities around them. From family members to casual acquaintances, the reactions of a grieving dad's community can have an enormous impact upon the success or failure of the grieving process.

Some of the responses from a grieving dad's community, however strained they may be, are actually helpful. Others cause harm. Sometimes, there is harm that is long lasting or in the worst cases, irreparable. But in almost all instances, it is safe to say that the things a grieving dad's community does and says will have a variety of potential effects — largely because the "perfect" thing to say to one grieving dad is exactly the *wrong* thing to say to another.

How then, should the friends, co-workers, and families of grieving dads respond to such awful circumstances? The answer, it seems, is just as elusive as the healing process itself.

Take for example the case of Frank, a 61-year-old Vietnam veteran. Frank's 21-year-old daughter, Rebecca, was the victim of a single-car accident not far from the family's home. In an ugly twist of fate, Frank was unfortunate enough to come upon the scene of Rebecca's accident. He arrived alone, aghast at the sight and in a state of shock over the absence of an ambulance, police cars, or anyone else for that matter.

When I think about that, it brings terrible images to mind. The strange familiarity of the car up ahead in the distance. The recognition that it is indeed the car of a beloved daughter. The realization that the car is in very bad condition, and the dreaded, reluctant walk to the wreckage.

And finally, the discovery that will mark the end of one life and a bunch of irrevocable changes to many other lives.

Frank's dreaded walk to the wreckage indeed revealed what he somehow already knew to the very core of his existence. His Rebecca had not survived the crash, and he responded the way every father would in such circumstances. He held his daughter close, no doubt trying with all his will to find a way to trade places with her, to protect his little girl one last time, even if it meant he'd have to die himself to do it.

Frank didn't call 911 right away. He knew that Rebecca had already passed on. His next move may seem strange to many who have no point of reference for being in such a situation, but to a grieving dad, it was a move that made perfect sense given its desperate context.

He picked Rebecca up, took her home, calling 911 later, and only when he was ready to do so.

That was in 2006. Today, Frank and his wife still have to drive by the scene of the accident each morning on their way to work. They now carpool together because driving alone is too difficult.

Many of Frank's friends and associates have stopped calling and talking to him altogether. In Frank's words, "They think that losing a child is contagious."

Hmm. Sounds familiar.

Others in Frank's community have expressed wonder at the fact that Frank and his wife still go to the cemetery to visit Rebecca every day. They don't understand that this is their way of grieving and remembering. "It's a void that can't be filled," Frank reflects. "It doesn't get better, but it gets easier."

"Easier," of course, is relative.

"People say you should be over it by now," Frank said in my interview with him. "It's easy for them to say. They haven't lost a child."

Some people in Frank's circle have told him that he "still has three other children," referring to his 35-year-old and his set of 33-year-old twins. As if that should somehow take the pain away that results from the loss of Rebecca. Simply put, he would carry his pain regardless of which child he lost.

Like many people who know a grieving dad, some in Frank's community look for the right words of comfort to deliver. This is a challenge that caring people try to meet all over the world every day — but one that is all but fruitless. Frank's take on this particular subject is simple. He says, "You don't have to say anything to 'fix' this problem. It is a problem you can't fix." Instead, it's a situation that calls for compassion and understanding.

Usually, the "understanding" part of that equation can only come from others who have experienced the loss of a child. Besides his immediate family, which seems to understand his pain better than anyone else in his community does, Frank has benefited from the Compassionate

Friends organization. Compassionate Friends is an international non-profit entity with over 600 chapters in the U.S., and it was founded upon the very principles that Frank alluded to in his discussion with me. In short, Compassionate Friends came about when an insightful chaplain at a hospital in England put four grieving parents together and observed the support they gave each other. That support was far more effective than anything he alone could have provided.

'Insight like this is rare, but it's not really all that difficult to apply. Most of the grieving dads that contacted me seem to agree with the central reality that "understanding" someone else's grief is not something that can be "acquired" through outside observation. Rather, such understanding can only be gained through experiencing firsthand the loss of a child.

Such is the case, of course, for the motherly side of the grieving dad equation. The wife or partner of a grieving dad is indeed experiencing the death of a child firsthand, and accordingly, she has unwillingly acquired an understanding of the depths of such profound loss. However, that understanding doesn't always mean grieving parents completely comprehend each other's pain.

They say that men and women grieve differently, but I am not sure if that's because society expects men and women to grieve differently or if it's just the way we are wired.

Because we all grieve differently and in our own time, we are often "out of sync" with our spouses. In fact, most grieving dads report that their grief experience is really quite different from their wives. Ultimately, that difference is responsible for a wide variety of strained responses.

Christine and I are really quite familiar — all *too* familiar — with the concept of being out of sync.

In the months that followed the death of our daughter, Katie, Christine and I were on very different paths with regard to our grief. I was on the path that most grieving dads find themselves following. If you need a hint, flip back to chapter three. I was the model "John Wayne," doing everything I could to be a "man," absorbing myself in things that could help me to avoid facing the trauma of losing Katie. And to top it all off, despite some episodes of complete physical and mental collapse, I thought I was doing quite well by embracing a strategy of refusing to look back upon something I couldn't change. I tried desperately to wrap up my pain into a nice little package and place it somewhere in a dark corner of my mind, never to be opened again.

Christine, meanwhile, wasn't doing well at all. By the end of January, which marked the third month since Katie's passing, it seemed Christine wanted to talk about what happened to our daughter every waking moment. It was the first thing we talked about in the morning. It was the topic of phone calls and e-mails throughout the day. Inevitably, as soon as I got home from work we picked up the conversation again. And naturally, it was the last thing we talked about before we fell asleep.

As time marched on, Christine became so consumed by our loss that she went into a deep depression and needed to take a leave of absence from work. She cried nonstop, and most days she simply stayed on the couch.

The worse off Christine became, the faster I tried to outrun the awful force that was eating her alive. I forced myself to get up and keep moving. I kept telling myself not to slow down or stop. But in reality, it was becoming extremely difficult to do all of this while my wife was held so firmly in the grip of her grief. And because I was doing such a bang-up job of ignoring my own trauma, over time I became resentful.

Finally, one evening I exploded, saying, "Could we please just have *one* moment that we don't talk about it?"

Christine just cried more. Like I said, we were out of sync.

From my perspective, this was not the Christine I knew. She was always such a strong, vibrant woman, equally driven at work and at play. A new fear began to set in on me. Was my wife going to be like this for the rest of our lives? Would I have to take care of her from now on? That was a frightening question to ask myself, because I was beginning to fear that I couldn't provide this level of support much longer. And dimly, I sensed that I couldn't keep fighting off my own grief while also helping Christine with her battle.

The solution was clear: I needed to become even busier. I took on additional work outside of my normal fifty-hour work weeks; soon I was working 60-70 hours per week. It felt good to be focused on something other than what had happened to Katie, even though I knew it was lurking somewhere deep down inside. And I knew that if I wanted to keep it buried, all I had to do was to continue moving.

When I was at work, it was easy to ignore my grief. I didn't talk to anyone about what happened and no one ever brought it up. My colleagues and I had an unspoken agreement: I was a guy, so I would toughen up and get through it, just as they expected it should be. And that's exactly what I was doing; I was pushing my sadness and grief away with all the strength I could find. Although it may have appeared as if I was doing okay on the outside, I was starting to crumble on the inside and the cracks in the facade were becoming harder to hide. I used one particular emotion to deflect all of this from being detected: anger.

Previously, I'd been one of the guys at the office who could be counted on to laugh and joke around. Now, I spoke only the minimum required to get a task done, and I became intensely focused on achieving my goals. I was on a mission to become successful, and if someone got in my way, I shoved him aside. I didn't have a concrete idea of what "successful" was, I just knew I had to keep moving. I was pissed off and it showed, sitting on a mountain of simmering rage.

A deeply buried part of me longed for someone to ask me how I was doing, but closer to the surface, I felt like I'd release my rage on anyone who dared to challenge me. I dared someone to do it — I was itching to lash out.

It didn't take long before my colleagues began to steer clear of me. Without realizing it, I was, in effect, alienating myself in my professional and personal life.

As is the case for many aspects of the grieving dad "experience," my strained responses and their consequences are not unique. Many grieving dads described similar circumstances in their own stories, especially when reflecting upon interactions with their colleagues.

Some of the best reflections about interactions within the community of a grieving dad's workplace have come to me from Joe, whose five-year-old boy, Joseph Jr., died late in October of 2009 after the H1N1 virus compromised his digestive tract, giving him a quarter-inch perforation in his intestines. According to the Center for Disease Control, this made Joseph Jr. one of 285 pediatric deaths attributed to the virus from April of 2009 to June of 2010.

Joe's son battled the virus for 10 days in the hospital, testing negative for H1N1 twice during that span. Doctors were at a loss to explain Joseph's condition, as the little boy went in waves from good to bad and back again. At 6:00 a.m. on the morning of the tenth day, things rapidly declined, and Joe got a call from his wife telling him that Joseph would need a respirator to breathe. Joe had stayed overnight at home with the couple's seven-year-old daughter and found some neighbors to watch her before immediately heading to the hospital.

By the time Joe arrived at the hospital, Joseph had crashed and it looked like a scene from *ER*, the doctors and nurses were working on him. All of this effort and they were unable to revive Joe's little boy, and after 45 minutes of trying, Joseph Jr. was pronounced dead.

For Joe, all of this was surreal. Just a few hours before, his son had made a face at his mother's attempts to feed him chicken broth. The child was sick, but he still had his wits and he was still maintaining his own stubborn ways — even with IVs attached to his arm after nine straight days in the hospital.

How could things deteriorate so fast?

Joe and his wife eventually grilled the medical team for over an hour, with questions regarding their son. Joe and his wife had done some research in the wake of Joseph's passing. No amount of research, however, could uncover the progression of what happened to their son. Joseph's doctors had done all they could.

Of course, that is of little consolation to Joe. In the five-plus months that followed Joseph's death, Joe Sr.'s interactions with his community of friends and colleagues were difficult at best, and fraught with a few very strained responses at worst. Especially at work.

"I know at work I've been a huge dick," Joe said in his interview with me. "I'll talk to someone and just chew them out. I don't know if it's that need to make someone feel as bad as I'm feeling."

One day at work, Joe was sitting at his desk with headphones on, listening to music and looking at pictures of his son. This was making him well up with tears, and at the time, he just needed to get away from everyone and be alone. One of his co-workers popped into Joe's office, looked at him, and said, "I think you need some sleep."

Joe told me that he wanted to say, "What the fuck does *that* mean? If I get some sleep, is that really going to change anything?" But he didn't.

In retrospect, Joe looks back on that time and realizes, most often, he tried not to judge people badly. He understood that those in his community were only trying to say something right — something, anything to help Joe through the most difficult time imaginable. But good intentions or not, clearly the interactions Joe has with workers become strained from time to time.

"There are deadlines and pressure at work, and people get short or snippy," Joe says. "I walk away. I've walked out of meetings."

When a colleague dared to ask where Joe was going, he took an "I don't give a shit" attitude. "If you have to fire me, *fire* me," Joe says. "I don't care. There are bigger problems in this world, and right now I think I'm facing the biggest."

Facing the loss of Joseph, has predictably also caused some strain in his marriage. But Joe and his wife have developed a healthy attitude toward each other's grief. In the early days following Joseph's passing, they established an understanding between each other that has resulted in the establishment of a few ground rules. Each of them has done well to recognize that the other has to deal with pain and grief in their own way. Sometimes, that means that if Joe needs to be by himself, it's okay for him to say, "Just get away, leave me alone right now."

"We've both said from the very beginning, that if I'm bugging you, if I'm pissing you off, tell me. Tell me to shut up. Be as rude as you want," Joe says. "My wife has a great analogy about that. It's like we're both on our own islands. We can see each other but we can't help each other. You want to, but you're going through your own shit."

Joe goes on to say he doesn't think these ground rules have brought the couple closer, but at the very least, the rules haven't divided them, either. There have been times when Joe or his wife has exercised the "leave me alone" rule, and although to someone on the outside such rules may seem harsh, they are working for them.

Joe's extended community has been helpful at times, too. Joe and his wife have a close group of friends that still invites them to parties and continues to include them as part of the circle. They don't accept every invitation, but they appreciate being invited and getting to make the decision themselves.

As an example of how different people respond to the same circumstances, my wife and I became pissed off at some dear friends when they extended an invitation to a wine party. I remember thinking, "A party? I haven't heard from you since our loss four months ago and now you decide to test the waters to see if I was ready to come out and play. My child died four months ago. The last thing I want to do is go to a party and act like nothing happened, because it did."

To continue with Joe's story, the passing of Joseph Jr. has also changed Joe Sr.'s outlook on life. As is the case with so many grieving dads, things that were important before his son died no longer seem important at all. And other things that weren't important before seem mission critical now.

"A guy I work with — his grandfather passed away — this was after Joseph passed away," Joe says. "He came back to work and I remember I walked by his office a couple of times and I thought, 'I need to go in there and say something.' I went in there and said, 'How are you doing? I heard your grandfather passed away and I'm sorry.'"

Joe says he never would have done that before Joseph died, but the grim understanding of grief that the loss of a child brings can be harnessed, in a way. In Joe's way, that understanding has led to a need for doing something more meaningful with his life — even if it's just to try and offer some comfort to a person that's going through a difficult time.

On a bigger scale, Joe and his wife have done their best to help people comprehend the dangers of the H1N1 virus. In March of 2010, a local television news station reached out to the couple and asked if they would be willing to talk about H1N1, because the "hype" surrounding the virus and the development of vaccines had died down. They agreed, and according to Joe, it turned out to be an excellent piece. They have also continued as advocates for flu vaccinations.

The experiences that Joe and his wife have been through offer a number of important lessons for the grieving dad. From the time that Joe left the hospital on the day Joseph died, he knew that help for grieving dads would be limited at best. Joe recalls that a hospital worker sent the couple away with some self-help materials. Joe's wife got a whole stack. For Joe, there were a few paragraphs that amounted to about half of one pamphlet.

Still, the "self" part of self-help is a relative thing, and one that Joe has engaged to the best of his ability. His best advice is to be sure to offer respect to your child by talking about him/her; in his own case, that means that Joe remembers the five and a half great years that Joseph was here. So he talks about his son. He laughs about his son. He discusses the things Joseph did to piss him off, and he talks about all the things he loved about him, too. And most importantly, Joe honors his son in one additional, significant way: by simply saying his name.

That tactic — the saying your child's name thing — works for some dads and triggers pain in others. In my situation, it seems to be a mixture of both. Sometimes, saying Katie or Noah's name is therapeutic. Other times, it brings to mind the things my children will never get to do, and along with that, it brings my pain to the surface all over again.

You know, some of the feedback I've gotten since I started writing this book suggests that since my children both died before they were born, I didn't have the time to "get attached." As if, therefore, my grief is somehow less valid than someone who has lived with a child for some period of years. My answer? Anyone who thinks that losing a child to miscarriage, stillbirth, or SIDS is somehow "easier" has never lost a child to miscarriage, stillbirth, or SIDS. This isn't a game of "my loss is worse than yours." It's the death of a child.

Period.

You don't have to take my word for it. You can get some "valid" perspective from Steven, who lost his 2-month-old son, Colin, to SIDS in 2011. It happened when Steven and his son fell asleep together on the couch. Steven had set a pillow underneath his arm to create a little crook for Colin to lie in, the boy's tiny body fitting perfectly within it.

"I always made sure his neck wasn't kinked or anything," Steven recounts. "I nodded off a little bit. It felt good to be close to him. I woke up in the exact position I was laying in. I thought he was still okay in the exact same position."

Nothing was disturbed, and Colin hadn't budged at all during Steven's brief snooze. He dozed in and out for the next 15 minutes or so, and when he was ready to get up, Steven followed his usual procedure for moving Colin off his chest during their little napping sessions. He started by sliding Colin down, which was the best way to move him without waking the little boy.

This time, though, Steven saw his son's head fall back.

"When I looked down, [I thought] 'okay, his head is fine.' But when I moved, his head tilted because he was dead at that point and there was no physical support coming from him at all."

Steven knew there was something horribly wrong. He saw the characteristic mix of blood and milk coming out of Colin's nose. He realized his son wasn't breathing, and he yelled upstairs to his wife, Elise, who immediately called 911 and administered CPR. Shortly thereafter, paramedics and police showed up at their house, and Colin was rushed to the hospital with his mother riding along in the ambulance.

Steven stayed behind at the house with the couple's young daughter, Allie, and two cops from the local police department.

Like in most states, by law, any infant death in a home has to be investigated. For Steven, that meant these two local cops were going to be in his face during the most difficult moments of his life. Looking back, Steven says he understands they were just doing their job, but he lost all respect for his local police department just the same.

"I know they have a job to do and the job is to make sure there is no abuse and the child is protected," Steven told me in our interview. "I was holding Allie. My arms are wrapped around my daughter, I'm bawling my eyes out, and I'm in a closed room. The only place I could go was to jump out a window and I'm only going to fall about 12 feet. I'm really not going anywhere."

The presence of two imposing police officers, coupled with the confusion and chaos that followed Colin's condition and the 911 call, frightened little Allie.

"My daughter's terrified," Steven recalls telling the cops. "She doesn't know you from anybody. Can't you stand out in the fucking hallway?" he pleaded. But the cops wouldn't budge — not even after Steven made the point that they had guns and could easily shoot him if they were worried he was some kind of threat. They stayed right there in the room with Steven and his horrified little girl, peppering him with questions the entire time.

Before long, the telephone rang, and it was Elise calling from the hospital to tell Steven that Colin had been officially pronounced dead. Nevertheless, one of the cops still persisted with his questions, even while Steven was trying to console his inconsolable wife over the phone.

"Shut the fuck up," Steven told the officer. "I'm getting a call from my wife that my son just died. I'll deal with you in a few minutes."

Those unforgettably horrifying moments were just the beginning of the continuing ordeal. First, there was the requirement that Colin undergo an autopsy. This would mean that for Colin's funeral services, the director would have to pin part of the sheet wrapping Colin up in a certain way, because the child's head would need extra support. Without it, Steven was informed that Colin's skull could fall apart due to the horrors of the invasive autopsy process.

"Can you imagine picking up your kid and having his head just collapse?" Steven reflected.

Later, there would be visits from the medical examiner. Child Protective Services would come to the house, too. In fact, the first time CPS showed up, Elise was sitting in Colin's room, writing a note to her son. It said that she wanted to join him.

Eventually, CPS could see that their daughter was in no danger, and they finally left the couple alone to face their grief in relative peace. For Steven, that has led to the typical roller coaster ride of emotions, from shock and denial to despair and anger.

The "anger" part is nothing new to Steven. Because of the rocky childhood he experienced, Steven was determined to give his son a far less angry environment than the ones he had experienced. As a child, Steven would come to know three different "fathers," each of which seemed progressively more abusive than the last.

It began with his biological father, who beat Steven recreationally for years. One time, when Steven was just 11, his dad beat him so severely that Steven's elbow was dislocated. Steven responded by sinking a lawn dart three inches deep into his father's thigh.

Even earlier, Steven experienced the responsibility of having keys to the family's home at the ripe old age of seven. By the time he was eight, Steven knew how to mix drinks. He also often got high. "I did a lot of things I wasn't supposed to," Steven recalls.

When Steven's mother finally divorced his biological father, she moved on to a second husband that was verbally abusive. She put up with that for a period of time, then found an alcoholic to marry for round three. At that point, Steven was 16 years old and he'd had just about enough.

One day, Steven was relaxing in the living room with his feet up on the coffee table. Husband number three didn't like that for some reason, so he came over and physically kicked Steven's feet off the table. That was the breaking point for Steven, and he told his stepfather that he could make a choice.

"You can get the shit kicked out of you in the house or out of the house," Steven told him. Then, he thought about that for a moment, and decided that outside would be better after all. "In the house, I have to clean up the mess, so let's go outside."

They went outside. Steven beat the hell out of him. All part of a regular day for a young man being introduced to the rest of his life with a new "father figure" to lead the way.

These experiences, however awful they may have been, taught Steven exactly how *not* to be when he eventually became a father. They also make it hard for Steven to forgive himself for what happened to Colin, because he's been fighting his own personal history in an effort to avoid repeating the mistakes.

"Shit, I just failed absolutely miserably," Steven says. "I couldn't help but feel that way."

Those feelings of failure — however misplaced they may be — are thoroughly mixed with guilt, too. What if Colin had been sleeping with Elise that night? What if Steven had tilted his son's head just a micro-millimeter in a different direction? A million what-ifs. But now, Steven recognizes that if his son was going to die, at least he died with one of his parents. And at the very least, Colin's last living contact wasn't with a mattress. It was with his father instead.

In addition to battling with guilt, anger, and his past, Steven faces ups and downs in his marriage. "We've had some of the most knock-down, drag-out fights in our marriage because the intense feelings mount in negative ways," Steven says. "There are moments every single day that I want to put a fist through a wall. And my wife has no clue what that is — she's like, well, 'Why would you want to hit a wall?'"

"It's a guy thing," Steven says.

"We've also had some of the most tender moments we've had in our marriage," he continues. "We're more aware of each other, closer, more accepting of the idiosyncrasies that used to drive us crazy."

Some of Steven's extended community of friends and co-workers are more aware, too. Steven is fortunate to have a few, in particular, who have helped him to face things head on, in an unapologetic yet insightful way.

For example, one of Steven's uncles called him in the months following Colin's death, and said he wanted to take Steven to a baseball game. The uncle did this in response to Steven's request to avoid asking him to make decisions. "If you want me to do something," Steven told his uncle, "then call me up and I'll come. If you make the effort, it will mean a lot more than asking me to make the effort." So Steven's uncle did exactly that, and the two of them went to a game, where Steven could take a little time to enjoy both his uncle and a little baseball.

Unfortunately, when the two of them got back to Steven's car after the game, they noticed that someone had put a few deep scrapes in the paint on the vehicle's back quarter panel. The next morning, Steven took another look and was about as pissed off as he could be. But just as other grieving dads have communicated, such things tend to pale in comparison to the trauma of losing a child, and before long, the damage to the car didn't matter so much anymore.

"About a week later," Steven told me, "I looked at it and the scrapes didn't seem all that bad. It's scrapes of paint — that's all it is. When I have some time, I'll take care of it. But right now, plastic doesn't rust."

One of Steven's friends, on the other hand, has a patently different perspective about the importance of cars. The friend's $70,000 BMW was badly damaged in an accident, but he wasn't seriously injured. When the friend expressed how distraught he was over working so hard for that car only to have it wrecked, Steven reminded him that the car was just made of rubber, plastic, sheet metal, and glass. The friend, who doesn't have children, didn't understand that line of thinking. Steven tried to put it into perspective for him: "At least you can *replace* a car."

As for his career, Steven has experienced more of the proverbial roller coaster ride. Some of it has been surprisingly positive. For example, one day when Steven was walking to his car, a fellow NASA colleague, by the name of Mark, stopped Steven in the parking lot and asked him how he was doing. Steven offered the obligatory, "Okay," and started to move on. Mark, however, wasn't buying Steven's bullshit, so he grabbed Steven's arm and said, "No. I didn't ask you to hear 'okay.' I know you're not okay. *How are you doing?*"

To Steven, that meant a ton. Mark took the time. He called Steven to the mat and didn't take the easy route by letting him get away with, "okay." Now, Steven considers Mark to be more of a friend than just a co-worker.

Others at Steven's office haven't been quite so "insightful." One in particular "almost joined Colin," Steven says, when the co-worker made the comment, "Think on the bright side. You are saving around $1,100 a month," referring to day-care expenses.

All of us have had our share of insensitive comments, but that one may win the prize for the worst possible thing anyone could say to a grieving dad.

As for the rest of Steven's community, there has been more of the same, predictable ping-pong match between positive and negative responses. His brother, for example, has been prone to making empty promises. Steven called him on it one day, telling the brother, "You can't keep telling me you're going to do x, y, and z and then not show up."

Steven's mother has contributed to the negative side of community reaction, as well. When she told Steven that she knew "exactly how you feel. I almost lost you," Steven reminded her that the operative word was, "almost."

"Here's the difference between what you went through and what I went through," he told his mom. "I'm your son and I'm sitting here 41 years later talking to you. My son and I won't have this conversation. Stop doing the 'almost' or 'exactly' how I feel thing — because you don't."

A worse example of "exactly" came from another member of Steven's community, who said, "I know how you feel. I had a parakeet die in my hand when I was young."

A *parakeet?* Really? You can buy a brand new parakeet at the store for about ten bucks!

Parakeets. BMWs. Day-care savings. These are just a few examples of the kinds of things grieving dads encounter in their daily interactions with the communities that surround them.

However, for every story a grieving dad can tell you about the negative side of community response, there's an offsetting story about a positive one. That is a very fortunate thing indeed, because without it, many grieving dads would hunker down and withdraw to the relative comfort that solace seemingly provides.

To be sure, solace is sometimes just what the doctor ordered. Other times, though, it's exactly the opposite of what a grieving dad needs. And for all of the things that a grieving dad's community might say to trigger an unhappy thought or the desire to put a fist through a wall, thankfully there are the Marks of the world, too. They are the part of a grieving dad's community that offers a sometimes blunt — but nearly always refreshing — form of communication that helps to keep us sane in the face of otherwise impossible circumstances.

CHAPTER 5

ROCK BOTTOM

AT ONE POINT in the middle of the fog that encased me after Noah died, it occurred to me that I was dying right along with him and his big sister, Katie. And you know what? I welcomed the possibility.

Although I wasn't suicidal, by late 2006, I had truly reached rock bottom, and I simply didn't care whether I lived or died. At this newest, lowest point in my journey through the passing of my children, my body was falling apart and I began to worry that my sanity was, too. I had become a shell of myself, someone I didn't recognize.

One day after calling in sick to work because my anxiety and sadness had gotten the best of me, I found myself on my hands and knees on the living room floor, begging God to help ease the overwhelming agony I was feeling. This was becoming something of a ritual for me; I was spending part of every morning praying to Him privately and intensely, pleading with Him to give me *just five minutes without pain.*

That kind of relief never seemed to show up on command, but I was hopeful that if anyone could help, maybe God could.

At this point in my life, this once confident, productive, and generally happy person now found himself having extreme anxiety issues. Simple tasks such as attending meetings for my job would cause me to panic. Meetings that I used to have no trouble navigating through prior to the deaths of my children, now terrified me for fear that I'd have an emotional breakdown in front of clients and coworkers. I had lost hope, drive, and confidence, and it was replaced with deep despair and unexplained fear. I had become someone I didn't know, seeing sides of me that I didn't realize I had. As the months went on, the toll that all of this stress had taken on my body was becoming obvious. This was a different kind of stress than what I had been used to in my job — this was *real* stress that would not let up. It was consuming every part of my life.

It was killing me ever so slowly.

During that time, no matter how hard I tried, I couldn't find a way — *any* way — to get the loss of my children off my mind. I had become obsessed and consumed with thoughts of their deaths. I started to see changes in my physical features. I dropped down to my lowest weight since college, my jawbone became defined (as in visible for the first time in years) and the material on my pants began to overlap under my belt because of rapid weight loss. I just wasn't hungry, and the thought of eating, often made me gag. I consumed only what was necessary, and retained the absolute minimum in order to function and survive — which usually consisted of a smoothie because I couldn't eat solid foods without throwing up.

All of the things I used to love and crave now had no place in my appetite. The lines on my forehead and around my eyes became more pronounced. My hair turned gray around the edges practically overnight. I was dying inside. Nothing, it seemed, could change that. The upbeat attitude and naivety I once had was gone, replaced now with the beaten down, weathered shell of a man I no longer recognized.

This I couldn't accept. I had never been so scared in my life. I was out of control and starting to realize I needed help. This was not something I could live through alone.

Finally, I gave in and decided to make an appointment with my family doctor. When I stepped into his office and he closed the door, he asked me what was going on, and before he got the words out I had already started to break down emotionally. I told him what I had been dealing with, and his diagnosis was quick and to the point.

It wasn't what I wanted to hear, to say the very least. My doctor told me I was suffering from depression brought on by complex grief. He tried to write me a prescription for an antidepressant, and he handed me the business card for a psychiatrist he wanted me to call.

But I didn't believe I had depression. No, depression was for weak people — and I wasn't weak! So I told my doctor I wasn't going to take the medication and wasn't going anywhere near a shrink.

That thinking lasted for almost a whole day. Almost, but not quite. Less than 24 hours after my "manly" declarations about shrinks and pills, I found myself in so much pain that I gave up, called the psychiatrist — and was promptly told he couldn't see me for almost a month.

A month? I wasn't sure if I was going to make it to the next day. A month just wasn't going to cut it. So I took control and called around until I found a counselor who could see me within a couple of days. I already had the prescription from my doctor, and it wasn't mandatory that I see the psychiatrist. I just needed to talk.

After I nailed down an appointment with the counselor, I headed to the drugstore to fill my prescription. When I got home with the medicine, I sat at the kitchen table with a pill in my hand, debating about whether or not to take it. Everything I ever was, seemed to be folded up into that little pill. Everything I ever *thought* I was, seemed to be at risk, if for no other reason than the notion *I* could possibly *need* such a pill.

I was scared, but I finally took the damn pill. After I swallowed it, I was convinced I had let myself down by not being strong enough to deal with this on my own.

The same thing happened at the counselor's office. I sat in the waiting room, hiding all of the tears I was crying and feeling ashamed that I was there to "talk" about my feelings. What would my family and friends think of me? This once strong, confident, "life of the party" guy had finally gotten so low he needed help. He gave in, closed down, and was doing something that he had always thought he never would.

A rock-bottom moment for me, for sure.

I'll come back to my own encounter with rock bottom later, but for now, most of the grieving dads I've interviewed can relate to what I'm saying here. There is a point for most of us that we can identify as the "bottom." It's that darkest of places that represents the very worst of our experiences. But just as it is with other things in life, finding "the bottom" is the only way to discover the path back to the top.

That, my friends, is the whole point of the stories you will read in this chapter.

We'll start with Scott.

Scott's son, Heath, was killed in action on November 22, 2006, as he was conducting operations against insurgents during his tour of duty as a Marine in Iraq. As with many of the soldiers killed in Iraq, Heath was taken by a roadside bomb. He was just 19 years old.

A lot has happened in Scott's life since then, and plenty of it has the hard and unforgiving feel of rock bottom.

First, there would be the dreaded news that all parents of children serving in active duty war zones fear the most. It starts with silence, ironically enough. In Scott's case, there would be a letter from Heath on October 28. Then nothing at all.

Nothing, that is, until November 22 — the day before Thanksgiving in 2006. A car pulled up in front of Scott's home. Two Marines got out.

"It was like you see on TV," Scott would tell his local newspaper, in an interview. "They come up to your house and you just know."

Spending that first Thanksgiving with the knowledge that his son was dead would mark the beginning of Scott's journey along the path to rock bottom. Despite the overpowering shock and trauma brought on by the news of Heath's death, the family did its best to celebrate Thanksgiving in a way that would honor Heath's memory. They did so privately, turning away reporters who were looking for holiday interviews.

But soon after — too soon from Scott's perspective — it would be time to bury Heath. The thought of putting his son in the ground, never to see him again, became too much for Scott to handle as the reality of this crushing loss began to settle in.

"I found myself panicking the morning of his burial," Scott told me. "I was absolutely scared shitless, absolutely just frightened at the fact of putting his body in the ground and covering it up and never, ever seeing this person again. I just could not comprehend that."

Unsure of exactly how he was supposed to proceed, Scott called a friend by the name of Karen, who could offer some unique perspective. She was his tax client, and she had experienced the death of two children — an 18-month-old to pneumonia, and a 25-year-old to suicide.

"She said, 'What are you afraid of?'" Scott recalls. "I said, 'I just can't put him in the ground like this. I don't know how you do this. How does a parent do this?'"

Karen told Scott that he essentially didn't have a choice. He had to do it. She told him that he had to dig deep, pull himself together, and bury his son. It was going to happen on that day. There was nothing Scott could do about it.

So, Karen reasoned, do it with dignity.

Dignity, it seems, would repeatedly become an issue in Scott's life as he struggled through the aftermath of Heath's death. Stay with me. You'll see what I mean in just a bit.

As Scott puts it, when there is a military death, there is a lot of, well, "pageantry." There is a lot of media attention, and a grieving dad who has experienced one of these "military deaths" soon comes to understand that there is a very public component to the early process of grief.

Part of that public process in Heath's case involved interment at Arlington National Cemetery. What could be more dignified than that?

Again, stay with me. More to come on that subject later.

When Heath was just 12 years old, he visited Arlington National Cemetery during a family vacation to Washington, D.C. Heath was awed by the experience, and he knew from an early age what his calling in life would be. Heath told his parents that he would be a Marine one day. He made that commitment a reality shortly after graduating from high school, and wound up serving about 18 months before the roadside bomb would ultimately take his life.

Scott's friend, Karen, was right, of course. Scott didn't have a choice, and Heath was indeed buried at Arlington National Cemetery, the military's pageantry in high evidence all along the way. When Heath's body was finally returned to the United States, there would be a funeral procession through the streets of his hometown that would include a horse-drawn carriage serving as a hearse. The media, their cameras and their microphones, were in high evidence, too, during all of this. Scott and his wife did their best to be gracious.

But all of it was happening so fast, and for Scott, that meant he would be dealing with a lot of "firsts" in a very short period of time. Many grieving dads have talked with me about the concept of "firsts," which reveals itself in the form of milestones that we have to overcome as we move through the months following the death of a child. In Scott's case, this was a magnified phenomenon, because he had to suffer the first Thanksgiving without Heath just one day after the news of his death. The first Christmas would come 13 days after his burial at Arlington. Then New Year's Day. And the day after New Year's Day, Heath's birthday.

That's a lot of firsts, and they left Scott feeling completely drained and emotionally numb. Eventually, "numb" led to some decidedly rock-bottom choices.

"I used my meds, used alcohol, and went through a very dark period," Scott told me. "Work was important but it really could not be the priority. I had a family that I was trying to keep together. My family had to be the priority."

Even at that, the pressures at work and the devastating shock of Heath's death were wearing Scott out at an alarming rate. He lost weight, and the generalized anxiety problem he had before Heath's death went into hyperdrive afterwards, spiraling out of control and leading to depression. At that point, which came about six months after Heath died, Scott knew the visits to his family doctor were no longer going to cut it.

"It was way beyond his ability to treat me," Scott says. "Not that he didn't try, but I had just gone down such a dark road that I needed a professional who could give me a diagnosis and treat me."

So Scott tried counseling, with mixed results. He says that it helped him to make better decisions instead of clinging to the rock-bottom kind, but it did nothing to take the pain away. In fact, one of the counselors he saw had a peculiar way of trying to help Scott deal with his anger. She had him write down the people and the things that were making him angry — not on paper, mind you — but rather she had him write on eggs. Then, she took him out to a field, where he was supposed to scream and throw the "offending" eggs as far as he could.

Like I said, mixed results.

At another point, shortly after George W. Bush left office, Scott wrote the former president, thanking him for his service to the country. In the letter, Scott told him about how he and Heath had attended a presidential rally in 2004, as well as the fact that the two of them had the privilege of shaking Bush's hand that day.

His reward? A mass-produced photo of Laura and George at the inauguration. No letter. No signature. No, "I am sorry for the death of Heath." To Scott, this was a real slap in the face. This was how his son's Commander in Chief would thank Heath for *his* service?

That little episode would wind up being the one time Scott found the egg-throwing to actually be therapeutic. "I was so mad, and I took that picture and I had my egg and it was my George Fucking Bush egg, and I threw it at his picture." It helped. Looking back, Scott says it's the one thing he laughs about most regarding his counseling.

Again, mixed results. Maybe I should head to the store for a dozen eggs.

The stress of everything from military pomp and circumstance to media attention and George W's snub has taken a heavy toll on Scott's family life. He is watching his remaining sons hit the proverbial reset button on their own grieving processes. When they were younger (Alex was seven, and Jeremy, 14, at the time of Heath's passing), they comprehended the grief the best they could. As they grow older, they have to reprocess the grief as they begin to understand it from their new perspectives.

For Jeremy, it's becoming increasingly difficult to live under the shadow of his fallen brother and all of the talk about Heath's heroism. Scott says that as he memorializes Heath, it's easy to forget that he has to be there for his living children, too.

"We give our heart, soul, mind, and being into raising our children," Scott reflects. "And when you lose a child it's like there's something torn out of you and I can't expect another son to understand how it is for me as a dad. I don't know what it feels like for him. But I can see that my actions hurt him."

Scott went on to say that he didn't realize he was hurting his family members because he was so caught up in his own grief. Like many grieving dads I've talked with, as well as a few that Scott has contacted over the years, we sometimes think that our own grief is worse than anybody else's.

"That's a hard thing for our family members to understand," Scott told me. "It really isn't that our grief is worse than theirs, it's just we get so lost we don't know how to process our feelings and it comes out like that."

Scott has tried to explain to Alex and Jeremy that to him, it's important that people don't remember Heath as just another soldier who was killed in Iraq. Scott wants Heath's legacy to be more than that, and he wants people to know him as being a light-hearted, country-serving, wonderful, and loving person.

There is dignity in that. More dignity than the rock-bottom experience Scott would have to endure as a result of confusion over Heath's burial. To understand what I mean, we go back for a moment to Arlington National Cemetery.

In June of 2010, three and a half years after Heath was buried, a report from the Army inspector general indicated that over 200 graves at the cemetery were either unmarked or misidentified. Worse, a Senate sub-committee investigation reported that as many as 6,600 soldiers buried at Arlington could be involved.

This, in and of itself, was upsetting enough. But layer on the fact that there were some inconsistencies in the Army's paperwork related to Heath, and the situation took on a whole new light. Specifically, Heath's documentation reflected that his funeral was held in Illinois rather than in Ohio. It also identified him as a Protestant rather than a nondenominational Christian, which was what Heath had indicated on his original documents when he joined the Marines. Further, it came to light that Heath's body had been stored in Virginia for several days before being transferred to Arlington, but his remains were not accounted for during the entire time of that transition.

All of this uncertainty led to serious doubts in Scott's mind, quite to the point that he decided dignity could be served only through doing something that could be viewed as patently undignified by some. He would travel to Arlington with his wife, and have his son's body exhumed. To Scott, it was the only way they could be sure that Heath was really there.

As Scott and his wife sat nearby, Arlington officials opened Heath's gravesite and his casket along with it. They managed to match ID tags at that point: one in the pocket of Heath's dress blues, and the other affixed to the casket itself. Still, there were doubts, so Scott asked them to look for the tattoo that his son had on one of his arms.

"I know it sounds crude," Scott told reporters. "But they had to dig for his arm because of the state of the body. I had them clean his arm, and I was able to verify his kanji, and I knew then it was Heath, for sure."

A kanji is a form of Japanese writing that uses Chinese characters. Seeing it on Heath's arm was the one sure way to bring dignity back where it belonged.

Scott publicly called for additional investigation into the matter. He went so far as to suggest that tourism be temporarily suspended at Arlington until all of the issues surrounding dubious gravesite identification were resolved.

Despite all of the additional anguish brought about by the uncertainty of Heath's burial at Arlington, Scott has never wavered in his support of the American armed forces. After the nightmare of the exhumation, Scott told reporters that he wanted "to say to the families across America who have lost loved ones and to those families who have brave men and women in service to the country — on behalf of a grateful nation, we thank you for your service and sacrifice. We honor your family and your loved ones."

Once more, plenty of dignity there.

Today, Scott continues to honor his son's memory through a blog he writes and a website dedicated to Heath and his life as a true American hero. These two sites offer Scott some solace, because of the knowledge that Heath's legacy continues to be recognized.

Additional solace sometimes comes to Scott, ironically, from Vietnam veterans. He's run across plenty of them during visits to Vietnam memorials. "I can go to a Vietnam memorial," Scott says. "I had a very nice bench made for Heath, and that's where I can go and sit. And sometimes the veterans will come up and sit with me and they'll talk with me." He goes on to say that the veterans he's spoken with seem to understand his loss, because they lost people they care about.

"I don't have to worry that they don't understand or they think I'm being a wimp or crybaby," Scott continues. "They've embraced me into their culture. They're my support people. They get it and I can talk to them about it."

After all he's been through, Scott is now a firm believer that peer-to-peer support is critical to surviving the loss of a child. He told me that he finds peer support to be the catalyst to help overcome the fact even as grieving dads learn to cope, we must understand that our child's death will be a part of our lives forever.

That part, whether you're "coping" or not, will never disappear. Instead, it will be a constant and dangerous reminder that rock bottom is never very far away.

Another grieving dad by the name of Sy can attest to that. Sy's 2½-year-old boy, Shaun, died in the summer of 2006, a victim of a drowning accident in a neighbor's swimming pool. Afterwards, Sy became something of a poster boy for the whole rock-bottom concept.

It started with anger. Lots and lots of anger. Sy found himself getting into fights, one of which was a verbal tangle with his boss in the weeks that followed Shaun's untimely passing. Sy was gainfully employed in the financial industry at the time, but after he told his boss to "fuck off," his days at the firm were over.

Fired and filled with angry despair over the cruel turn his path in life had taken, Sy turned to alcohol and drugs in his search for relief. He went on a rampage in that department, abusing pot, cocaine, and booze to the point where he'd wake up from binges completely clueless as to his whereabouts or how he'd gotten there.

"All I did was sleep, get up, drink, and pass out," Sy related to me in our interview. "I couldn't eat. I lost 30 pounds in a month."

This continued over the course of the two months after Shaun died, and as a result, Sy was hospitalized on three occasions. Following one particularly bad episode, Sy spent an entire month in the hospital, including several days in the intensive care unit. The doctors, Sy told me, were afraid he would have a heart attack.

"After Shaun died, I tried every day to die," Sy says. "I wasn't suicidal; I just didn't care if I died. I never thought I would be happy again. I never thought I would smile again."

After doing a stint in rehab and nevertheless continuing to drink himself into oblivion, Sy waded through his post-Shaun life in an alcohol-induced stupor. Eventually, all of this destructive behavior earned

Sy another notch in his rock-bottom belt, as his wife finally left him in 2009.

For Sy, his wife's departure was the catalyst that would finally wake him up. A few days after she left, Sy woke up one morning and decided he was done. He's been sober ever since.

How did he do it? How did he pull himself out of the cavernous depths of rock bottom and become interested in living again?

"I learned to live on *life's* terms," Sy told me. "One day at a time. I finally accepted my son's death, and recently celebrated Christmas for the first time [since Shaun died]."

In short, Sy decided to get his shit together and finally do something. He went back to school and got a bachelor's degree in legal studies.

He got a completely new outlook on life, too.

That attitude has carried over to his relationships as well. Sy met a new girl, whom he refers to as a "wonder woman." It's also made an impact on his careers; I say "careers," because now he has more than one. In addition to a new job he's grown to love, Sy also performs as a stand-up comedian. It's his way of bringing humor to others, while providing an outlet for the anger he still feels about Shaun's death.

"The pain still gets to me from time to time, but I know that's just the way it's going to be," Sy reflected. His standup routine, which doesn't include any references to Shaun's death, helps him to avoid dwelling on his own pain. He feels that's because he's providing his audience with a way to escape their problems, even if only for a few minutes.

Although nightmares and flashbacks still happen, Sy keeps them under control through his regular attendance at AA meetings, which have become the default forum for expressing what he's feeling about Shaun's death, and they have fortified his positive approach to life these days.

Still, there are the everyday encounters with people who just don't get it. When Sy hears people complaining about their "bad" day, he thinks, "You have no idea what a bad day really is." But when those same people say something that might have annoyed him in the past, now he takes a "Yeah, whatever" approach that he finds mentally liberating.

"Life has a weird way of turning around and healing wounds," Sy says.

When I asked him what advice he might give to other grieving dads who have had similar rock-bottom experiences, Sy said, "I would tell them that with help, you can get through it. How do they believe that? They just have to believe their child is with them and wanting them to survive. Let go of the guilt and anger and know that their child is looking out for them."

My sentiments exactly, Sy.

--

Looking back on my own worst memories of rock bottom in 2006, I now realize I was being way too hard on myself. My convictions about depression and its stigma as a disease for the weak was entirely misplaced. Depression isn't just for weak people — it's a real, dyed-in-the-wool health condition. Okay, so we can't get a diagnosis by submitting to a blood test, but depression is as real as any disease can get, and I have met some pretty tough guys that have also found themselves in the depths of the pain depression inevitably brings.

As men, we all like to think of ourselves as tough guys, and as a result, we sometimes let our pride get the best of us. Which, in turn, gets in the way of asking for help. Hell, most of us are too damn arrogant to ask for directions when we get lost; why would anyone think we'd ask for directions when we're suffering emotionally?

Well, by the time late fall of 2006 rolled around, I needed directions for sure. Fortunately for me, I wound up meeting a man by the name of Rick, who was a Stephen's Minister (someone who volunteered his time to help other men through difficult circumstances) at the church I occasionally attended with Christine. I told Rick the story of Katie and Noah, and he listened — I mean, he *really listened*, closely and with intense awareness of everything I had to say. He never broke eye contact, and his rapt attention alone was a real gift, especially compared to the dozens of people who studied the floor as they mumbled condolences while they "listened."

But Rick wasn't done with the gifts; besides his unique ability to remain actively engaged through some very tough subject matter, he still had one important gift left to give. It came in the form of five simple words

— words he delivered after I finished telling my story, and only after he sighed heavily, as if releasing some of the burden of carrying the weight of the world on his very own shoulders.

"That's a heavy load, brother," he said.

Those simple words would become the turning point in my struggle against the rock bottom of my battle with grief. Upon hearing them, I instantly felt a deep and visceral response to Rick's words, because at last, someone else — a *man* no less — had finally acknowledged that what I had gone through was incredibly traumatic stuff. He granted me permission to grieve without hiding behind a facade.

For me, hearing those words and letting my brain absorb their meaning was truly the start of my long, hard journey of healing. From that point on, I knew that although I was still in pain and probably always would be on some level, there was nevertheless a way back from rock bottom. The path, lined with the simplicity of recognition, was just as Rick suggested through the wisdom of those five uncomplicated words.

"That's a heavy load, brother."

For too long, men have suffered in silence behind the facade of strength that society has expected them to build. For too long, we've kept things bottled up, living with the mistaken assumption that real men don't complain or cry. I was certainly no different, having played the part of the "big boy" who didn't cry, ignoring my own pain in favor of dealing with my wife's and choosing to keep moving along instead.

But as I have come to learn — very much the hard way — playing the tough guy and keeping emotions bottled up is a fabulous recipe for becoming well acquainted with the concept of rock bottom.

One particular grieving dad, whom I've corresponded with, can tell us quite a bit about this whole rock-bottom thing. His name is Jody Dark Eagle Breedlove.

You might be saying to yourself, "Dark Eagle. That's an interesting name." Indeed it is — not only because Jody is an American Indian, but also because he is an interesting person to say the very least. His story is quintessential to understanding the rock-bottom experience of being a grieving dad.

Jody's story starts out like so many of the ones I've encountered during my discussions with grieving dads. There is a loving son, and his name is Taylor. The son is growing up, living with a beautiful girlfriend and a young daughter of his own. But the son has not forgotten the dad — not at all. They still see each other often. They play music together. They interact in the same ways they did when the son was a younger boy — living life together with a great sense of happiness and contentment. There is still the love between father and child, even if the son is moving through life the way a growing man normally does.

But "normal" went away one day when Taylor had an argument with his girlfriend, and to him it was awful enough that living didn't seem so full of contentment anymore. So Taylor took his own life, choosing to leave this world behind in favor of whatever is on the other side. He was only 19.

He might as well have taken Jody with him, because Jody's life, too, would never again be the same. Instead, Jody would become immersed in the life of a man who would find himself all but racing for rock bottom.

Once the successful owner of a construction company, Jody would lose it all — *everything* — in the months that followed Taylor's death. The decline in his business had started because Jody was injured when he fell from a roof. This occurred well before his son passed away, getting to the point where Jody was evicted from his home of 14 years — because he was two months behind on his house payments.

After his son was cremated, Jody continued to endure more hardship and misfortune. Ultimately, he would find himself homeless and living in the back of his pickup truck for nearly two years.

How's that for rock bottom?

In my correspondence with Jody, he has told me he believes anyone with the resources to get help after the death of a child should definitely do so. He finds it unimaginable that a father could possibly try to go it alone after the passing of a beloved son or daughter. In his own case, Jody had little choice but to forego professional counseling, because he didn't even have a *home,* much less the considerable dollars counseling can sometimes absorb. And since he now lives in a small, borrowed trailer in the woods of Colorado, support group resources are nowhere nearby, even if he had the wherewithal to pursue them.

Homeless or not, Jody is not content with surviving in the depths of a rock-bottom existence. Instead, he is using his pain and remarkable talent for writing to express the love he has for Taylor in a forthcoming book called *Enemy Ghost*. Thus Jody, who was homeless at the time he made connections with me, is working toward honoring Taylor's life through talking about his son in his very powerful and prolific writings.

Almost universally, the grieving dads I've spoken with have told me that talking about their children is a heavy-therapy antidote to the hefty loads we all carry. This, of course, was the thinking behind this book in the first place. Based upon my own experiences after the deaths of Katie and Noah, it seemed to me that an invitation to tell their stories might be all that most grieving dads would need to open up.

Many grieving dads who have followed my Grieving Dads blog have expressed that healing can be brought about simply by recognizing they are not alone in their grief. Telling their stories, it seems, offers a way to pick themselves up from rock bottom, hopefully to the point that further trauma for their families and loved ones can be avoided.

Tragedies such as divorce, alcoholism, drug dependence, job loss, nervous breakdowns, thoughts of suicide, and yes, even homelessness are all heartbreakingly common after the death of a child. They are all part of the formula for a rock-bottom existence, and to my way of thinking, their impacts can be minimized if not avoided altogether, as long as grieving dads are willing to embrace the notion that talking about their children will actually help. It also helps to have a willingness to allow others to help them carry the load when they can't carry it further themselves.

On that subject, the survey response I received from Bob comes to mind. In December 2009, Bob got a phone call from his son's fiancée. "There's been an emergency," she said. "You have to come immediately."

Bob made his future daughter-in-law tell him what was going on, even though somehow he already knew.

"Will is dead," she told him.

Will attended college about three hours away from his parents' home, and for whatever reason, he never woke up from the nap he took at his girlfriend's apartment that day. He had finished taking two final exams that afternoon, and when his fiancée found him, he was lying face down on the floor of the apartment. The cause is unclear; speculation includes everything from an allergic reaction to a choking episode.

Bob's first reaction was an angry one. He wanted to blame someone. Later, he realized that the three stark words his son's girlfriend spoke over the phone would change his life completely. Forever.

By the time Bob and his wife completed the drive to the hospital where Will was located — a drive that began with the knowledge their son was dead — it was 1:45 a.m. Just hours earlier, that same son sent an email to Bob. A little after that, Will called his mother, offering to do some Christmas shopping for his younger sister before he came home for the holidays.

Now, that same son was dead and alone, lying under a sheet in an empty room, just like in the movies.

Bob and his wife stayed with Will for several hours, until he became so cold to the touch that they couldn't even bend his toes anymore. Still, they didn't want to leave. When Bob and his wife tried to sleep that night, it felt like Will was right there in the room with them, trying to speak to them as a ghost.

"CHEATED," Bob wrote in his survey response. "I feel cheated out of the ballgames, dinners, and conversations that I would have with my son to talk about all the things we did and all of the things we were going to do. But most of all I feel cheated for him, because he will not be able to do them."

Based upon the interviews I've conducted with other grieving dads, the feeling of being cheated is a natural one. And when a man feels cheated, he is apt to look for someone to blame.

"I want to blame God, but God is my only window to see him again, so I really can't," Bob said in his survey response.

Other windows into the tragedy that take Bob toward rock bottom include drinking, apathy, and you guessed it, more anger.

"I drink more, and I don't feel bad about it. I no longer experience joy," Bob wrote. "I don't care what people think anymore, and I used to. Problems at work and home are insignificant to me — I really don't care if they are managed or not."

Sounds a lot like the same sort of rock bottom I've experienced.

As for the anger part, Bob can't help but feel some of it for Will's former fiancée.

"I don't hold her responsible, but she is the face I see when I replay the call," he wrote. "His fiancée is moving on with her life, and I'm angry that she can."

Again, I find this kind of emotion really quite common among grieving dads. I think anger is expressed more in men because it's the one emotion that society allows men to show. Crying, not so much. Although some "experts" might suggest that such anger is "misplaced," I would say otherwise. I'd say it's a perfectly natural response to the experiences grieving dads have endured. I've felt this emotion, especially related to how other people laugh, smile, go to work, watch ballgames, eat dinner, or even go to the bathroom — all the things my children will never do — yet the world just keeps moving along anyway.

Yes, indeed, the world has a not-so-funny habit of spinning on its axis in a maddeningly reliable way. Such was the case when the reality of Bob's situation hit home, and before he knew it, the time had come to bury his beloved son.

Over 1,000 people attended Will's funeral, and there were too many flowers for the church to hold. According to Bob, every teacher Will ever had — every principal, every coach, every girlfriend, and every girlfriend's parents came to the funeral. There was something very special about Will, and everyone he touched seemed to understand that.

"Every adult I ever met told me we had raised one of the finest young men they had ever met, and wanted to know how we did it," Bob wrote. "He had a plan, and it was on track. He was looking forward to work, marriage, and all of the challenges that he would face. He was excited about coming home for Christmas. He was a great kid."

By his own admission, Bob could go on writing about Will forever, which he does, in his journal.

It helps. Just like it's helped almost every grieving dad I've ever met. That's because the death of a child is so unimaginably hurtful — so fundamentally *devastating* — that any attempt by a grieving dad to hold his emotions at bay is fruitless at best, and a one-way ticket to rock bottom at worst.

For me, as difficult as it was to finally give in, take that pill, and to spill my guts to a counselor, it was the best thing I could have done. It allowed some of the pain to begin flowing out of me. Okay, maybe not all of it — far from it. But because I finally asked for help, I finally got some relief.

Today, I am such a believer in the counseling process that I'm putting my money where my mouth is and pursuing a Master of Education in Counseling. I hope to use what I learn through this process to help others navigate their way past the death of a child and back toward living meaningfully.

Trust me, I am the last person I ever would have thought would be a counselor, but who better to help someone up from rock bottom than someone who's been there?

Always remember: *"That's a heavy load, brother."*

You don't have to carry it yourself.

CHAPTER 6

REAL HELP

A GRIEVING DAD MUST face many hard truths after the death of a child, but for me, perhaps the most sobering one is the fact that I received more help from strangers than I did from people I knew.

Maybe that's why psychiatrists make so much money. After all, many of us are more comfortable talking about our problems to strangers than we are talking to friends or relatives. Alcoholics and gamblers, when you think about it, often find more real help in support groups like AA and GA than they do from their own families. Why should we think it would be any different when it comes to the death of a child?

Well, the passing of a child is "different" for sure, but there is one important constant that can't be denied. When people need help — *real help* — they are never very likely to find it within the confines of their own homes or the limitations of their own thought processes. Instead, people who need real help often don't get it until: A) they're willing to admit they *need* it; B) they seek it from sources outside the ones they know best; or C) they hit rock bottom so hard they don't know what else to do.

Coming from a man with an unfortunate amount of experience in this particular arena, I'm here to tell you it's the same for grieving dads. If you need a few reminders about why, flip back to chapter four. Yes, in chapter four you read plenty of positive things about the help grieving dads can get from their families and friends. But lest you forget, there is also lots in chapter four about how strained the relationships can be between a grieving dad and his existing community.

Don't get me wrong. I am not saying that a grieving dad shouldn't turn to his friends and relatives for assistance with his pain. Not at all. Nor am I saying that reaching out to a shrink, a counselor, or a support group is an absolute must for every grieving dad.

Enough about what I'm *not* saying. From my point of view, a grieving dad shouldn't stop with the people and places he already knows in his quest for real help. If I had done that — if I had relied exclusively upon my existing circle of friends and family to bring me back among the living — I don't know if I would have survived, period. It's important to surround yourself with people that have compassion and understand what you are going through. Oftentimes, people who are close to you just want the old you back so they try hard not to "bring up" the subject of your child who has passed away. In reality, sometimes all you want to do is talk about your child, so it's important to find someone who will listen, whether it's a stranger or someone that listens for a fee.

This I say because despite my attempts to "man up" and swallow the pain all by my macho self in the early going as a grieving dad, I now know that I couldn't have survived without the friends, family, co-workers, strangers, professionals, and support groups who reached back when I reached for them.

"Them" includes a long list of people to whom I will forever be grateful. There was Sarah, the hospital chaplain who was there with us when Noah died. Then there was Lynda, a dear friend who would reach out to me with tough love while coping with her own battles with breast cancer. My buddy, Brent, would take my call regardless of what he was doing at the time. The dear friends we met at support groups, and still have close relationships with, because they get it. My former co-worker, Jamie, who would willingly listen to my tear- and snot-filled pain every morning for almost a year. Finally, there was Rick, the Stephen's Minister of *"that's a heavy load, brother,"* fame who listened to my story with rapt attention and ultimately became the catalyst for my own healing process.

Some of the grieving dads I've interviewed in my travels got luckier than I did, because they found the holy grail of real help in one or two conspicuous places. But for most of us, real help comes in small doses, a little bit at a time, from a lot of different places and people.

I know that was the case for me. In my talks with a grieving dad from Chicago by the name of Kermit, it appeared to me that he shares the "small doses" philosophy of real help. I should have known before I even met him, because it took three months of email correspondence between us before he agreed to meet in person.

When the day finally arrived and the place was set, I found myself waiting 20 minutes beyond the appointed time, and I began to fear Kermit wouldn't show. Not that I could have blamed him. From CNN to online blogs, there was a lot of publicity surrounding Kermit's membership in the grim club of grieving dads.

That's because his son, Kermit Junior, became a murder victim in the city of Chicago in 2008. After taking a temporary hiatus from the 500 homicides milestone from 2004-2007, Chicago was once again the murder capital of America.

In addition to being one of over 500 murder victims that year, Kermit Junior was also counted among the 74 percent of African American victims (according to the *Chicago Tribune*), which means there were more black people killed in Chicago in 2008 than there were U.S. soldiers killed in Iraq that year.

Dubious, indeed. But as awful as the circumstances surrounding Kermit Jr.'s death, there was nothing dubious about his life.

From the time he was just a little kid, Kermit Junior wanted to be a basketball star. He reached for that dream a little at a time as he grew up, and after he graduated high school, he played ball for community colleges. Finally, in the summer of the year he was killed, Kermit Junior had the opportunity to have his skills tested on the courts of the 2008 NBA camp in St. Louis.

Those tests, Kermit Sr. was told, were off the charts. So much so, that his talented son was literally bombarded with coaches, scouts, and agents attending the camp. Kermit Jr. belonged on an NBA development squad, they told him. But unfortunately for his family and the NBA fans that would have enjoyed seeing him play pro ball, Kermit Junior's killers had different ideas.

It happened just one block from his home. Kermit Jr. was sitting in a car with three other people, parked at the side of the road as they waited for a guy that Kermit was supposed to play basketball with later in the day. When the guy finally showed up, he had another man in tow — one that neither Kermit nor the other passengers in the car recognized. Then, both of them tried to rob the driver, who resisted and attempted to pull away. One of the attackers started shooting, and Kermit Jr. was hit once, as was another passenger, who was lucky enough to escape with a minor wound to the elbow.

Kermit Jr., however, was not so lucky. He rolled out of the car and fell on the snow-covered ground, where a neighbor discovered him. The neighbor covered him in blankets to keep him warm until an ambulance could arrive.

For Kermit Sr., the memories of the day his son was killed will always be with him. He first got word from his youngest son, who called to say, "Dad, I just got this crazy phone call that Kermit got shot."

Kermit Senior's natural reaction was to call Kermit Junior's cell phone. When Junior didn't answer, Kermit hung up and his phone rang almost instantly. There was a stranger on the other end of the line.

"You don't know me," the stranger said, "but I got your phone number off a note on your front door that you left for UPS. I am calling you to tell you that your son has been shot. He is in the ambulance. He is moving and seems to be okay right now. I don't know where they are taking him."

The guy on the phone who was delivering this terrible news did his best to inform Kermit Sr. about which hospital the ambulance would be going to, but because of the nature of the crime, the paramedics wouldn't divulge that information.

So, imagine for a moment sitting stuck in Chicago traffic after learning that your son has been seriously wounded, and no one can tell you where he's being taken for treatment. Somehow, instead of panicking, Kermit Sr. had the presence of mind to call a friend who was a Chicago police officer. The friend was able to tell Kermit where to go, and when he arrived at the hospital, the news was not good. His son was no longer stable, and the hospital had dispatched a surgeon who had yet to arrive.

As Kermit Sr. relates all of this to me during my interview with him, he gets very quiet at this particular point of his story. Then, he tells me that before his son went into surgery, he had the chance to see Kermit Junior. He couldn't have known it at the time, but this would be the last chance he would ever have to talk to his son.

"I looked at him, and he was wincing from the pain," Kermit tells me. "I told him, 'Look, man, I need you to fight. I just want you to know that I love you, man. We're going to get through this. I am praying for you and I need you to pray. I need you to fight.'"

Kermit leaned over and kissed his son on the forehead. That kiss, along with Kermit's words of prayer and encouragement, were enough to help his son fight hard through the surgery.

Very hard.

When the surgeon finally came out of the operating room, he told Kermit that his son died and came back to life on three separate occasions during the surgery. He fought to stay alive, but the bullet that passed through Kermit Junior's liver also went through the ventricle of his heart. As the surgeon was saying all of this, tears were filling his eyes.

"He didn't make it," the surgeon told Kermit. "I did everything I knew to do." Then, the surgeon collapsed into Kermit's arms. Shortly after taking in the worst news he'd ever received in his life, Kermit Sr. went to see his son. "I saw him lying there and he looked like he was sleeping," Kermit tells me through tears. "I wanted to shake him. I thought, 'Lord, I don't get this. We were so close to him achieving greatness.'"

On December 28, 2008, over 3,000 people came to Kermit Junior's funeral. Capacity at the church was only twenty-two hundred, so there were many standing room only attendees. Mercifully, Chicago took a break from the homicide scene on the day of Kermit's burial. No one was murdered in the city that day, but nevertheless, there would be more victims killed after Kermit Junior in 2008.

Just one week prior to my meeting with Kermit, they arrested two men and charged them both in Kermit Junior's case after pulling them over for a routine traffic stop. They're still awaiting trial as I write this.

The news of the arrests was bittersweet for Kermit. He knows he will have to relive the nightmare all over again, just as he did immediately after Kermit Jr. was killed. Detectives were constantly stopping by the family's home to ask questions, so Kermit had to put the grieving process on hold. To make matters worse, Kermit says that everyone "pretty much knew who did it and what happened, but there wasn't enough evidence to make it stick."

But the streets of Chicago talk. Kermit listened, and he knew more about his son's fate than most grieving dads would ever want to know.

In between the detectives' questions those first four months that followed his son's death, Kermit reached into the Bible for counsel. For him, this was a natural place to turn, since he's involved as the minister of music for two large churches in the Chicago area.

One particularly helpful passage came to Kermit from Romans, chapter eight, verse 29:

> *"All things work together for good,*
> *for those who are called according to His purpose."*

As Kermit points out, it doesn't say, "all *good* things," it says, "all things."

The Bible wasn't Kermit's only source of real help. He also found it through a psychologist at his church, who invited Kermit to come and see him anytime he wanted. The psychologist told Kermit that he admired the work he'd done with the churches, and that he was happy to offer any help he could to Kermit and his remaining children. Kermit took him up on that, and started sessions with the psychologist about a month after Kermit Junior's funeral.

My interview with Kermit made a lasting impact on me. He helped to solidify my own convictions that grieving dads must seek help — real help — if they are to have any hope of overcoming the shattering pain of a child's death. One of the things Kermit said during our talks really hit home:

> *"God doesn't always reveal His plan,*
> *but He will reveal His next step."*

Kermit also told me that a pastor once had a profound thought that has brought some real help, too. He said, "If the why is big enough, the how doesn't matter." This made an impact on me as well, because at the time we met, I was still trying to figure out how I was going to bring this book to life so other grieving dads would have a resource. After mentioning this to Kermit, he made that statement. Those words motivated me to keep going because the "why" far outweighs the "how."

If you are reading this book, the "how" took care of itself.

I have a funny feeling that Kermit Sr. is going to make a lasting impression on lots more lives before he's finished with his own life here on earth. Kermit is one good dude and a father any kid would love to have as a dad.

--

Another grieving dad who believes in real help is Joe, a man I met in the summer of 2010 for an interview. Joe's son, Dan, passed away on Memorial Day weekend in 2005 after battling his whole life with Evans syndrome. He was 14.

Evans syndrome is a rare disease for which there is no known cure and no definitive agreement as to its causes. The disorder affects the immune system in a way that causes the manufacture of antibodies, which attack red and white blood cells as well as platelets. In Dan's case, the disease put him at risk for everything from anemia to major internal bleeding from simple bumps or bruises.

On that fateful Memorial Day weekend in 2005, the family was enjoying the holiday camping-style, when Dan started showing symptoms. Up to that point in his life, Dan had been in and out of hospitals as a matter of routine. His mother, Deb, who is an RN, became completely immersed in Dan's care over the years, going so far as to keep a journal in which she recorded every detail of her son's battle with the disease. Her little book included everything from chronological description of symptoms to vital signs and height, weight, or body temperature statistics. In this way, Dan's mother remained perpetually prepared to relate detailed information to doctors whenever the need for another trip to the hospital might arise.

On this particular occasion, which was the Saturday of the holiday weekend, Dan had a temperature and reported that he just didn't feel good. Joe's wife reacted as she almost always did, with the announcement that it was time to head for the hospital.

Joe, however, talked her out of it.

"I'm looking at her [and saying], 'We're having fun out here,'" Joe told me during our interview. "'Don't let the fever ruin it.'"

Deb listened. And then the very next day, when Dan got worse, she took him in after all. As they now know all too well, it would be the last time their son would ever spend time in a hospital room.

"That's another thing I can't get past," Joe tells me. "Now I feel guilty because I made Deb keep him home. She never, ever would do that. Well, Sunday he got real bad so she took him to the hospital and he passed away."

Dan hung tough until Tuesday, when he began coughing up blood. Since he was scheduled for a blood transfusion the next day, the medical staff at the hospital decided to keep him overnight. Unfortunately, things got even worse by Tuesday afternoon, to the point where a ventilator became necessary.

"We were talking [to Dan] just like this," Joe said, referring to the way he and I were carrying on our conversation. "They'll put you on a ventilator, make you breathe easier so when you wake up, you'll see Mom and Dad and you'll be fine."

Except he wasn't fine. He went into cardiac arrest and never came out.

To this day, the image of hospital staff pounding on his son's chest for an hour and a half is burned into Joe's memory. Along with the CPR, Joe also had to watch as the doctors continuously sucked blood out of Dan's lungs. All of it was useless in the end, and Dan passed away that afternoon.

"I could not get past that," Dan says. "That's why I try not to talk about it too much. It's tough."

For the first month after Dan's funeral, Joe went to the gravesite every day. He was becoming distant from his family, lost in the malaise that many grieving dads experience after the death of a child.

Joe's brother, who had no children, filled that particular void in his life through great relationships with Joe's kids. He took Dan's death very hard; he got sick and couldn't get out of bed. He had headaches, and when he could no longer summon enough motivation to go to work, Joe's brother finally consulted a doctor.

The first one he saw said there were signs of depression. Joe's brother dismissed the notion, and sought a second opinion. When the second doctor confirmed the diagnosis, Joe's brother finally gave in and accepted a prescription for medication.

Joe's brother saw the same signs in Joe that he had experienced. He knew Joe was having problems, and he was successful in talking Joe into going to see a doctor.

Enter real help.

"Depression medicine helped for a while," Joe told me. I could relate, since it had helped me too, even if it was only for a short time. No matter, though. Whatever gets you through the night, as they say.

As is the case for many grieving dads, Joe worries about his relationship with his wife.

Joe and Deb tried going to a marriage counselor for a little while. This, of course, is a common course of action for grieving parents — but not one that Joe was inclined to pursue long term. "It's like they're watching their timer," Joe said. "I stopped going."

At least they tried. My own wife refers to counselors as friends for a fee — but for me, it was money well spent.

Fortunately, the couple also tried another avenue in their search for real help. They began attending a local Compassionate Friends group, and therein found some success. Now he and Deb can see themselves in the faces of new people who come to the meetings. As a result, they've become witnesses to the fact that even though the death of a child is a catastrophic thing to endure, life can still get better.

You never get over it. But it does get better. Or as my wife and I say, "You get *through* it, but you never get beyond it."

Joe and Deb's marriage has gotten better, too. Their experiences with Compassionate Friends have helped teach them to encourage people to talk with them about their son. Now, Joe feels that if people are talking about Dan, then it must mean his son has made an impact in the lives of others.

To this day, Dan's friends still do just that. In fact, on the May 31, preceding my interview with Joe, three of them stopped by his home just to say they were thinking about Dan.

"It lifts you up," Joe says. "We know we did a good job with him. He was a good kid. A good friend to a lot of people."

Knowing that has to be among the best kind of real help a grieving dad can get, when you think about it. In my work with grieving dads, I have found that similar sentiments are quite common indeed. Nearly every dad I've received survey responses from or interviewed has indicated that when there's any hint of recognition that he's done a good job as a dad, it's universally helpful in dealing with the death of a child.

While I was meeting with Joe, the subject of work came up and we both talked about how difficult it is to go back to a job as if nothing has happened to you — because obviously, something has happened. Your stress level has changed and sometimes you have to seek help by changing jobs or move on to a career that is less demanding. Of course, I do not recommend doing this right away, but it may be something that enters the mind as you travel along this road. Making gradual changes in your life to reduce stress is something I have done. I know I am not the same person I was before, so why keep going as if nothing happened? Sometimes, however, in the interviews I've conducted, real help comes from less likely sources. Take the case of Jeff, for instance.

In July of 2010, I interviewed Jeff during the Bereaved Parents of the USA's national gathering in Little Rock, Arkansas. Since I was conducting one of my workshops at the event and Jeff was attending the event with his wife, we agreed that this would be the place to meet.

Jeff's 25-year-old son, Jeffrey, died in a motorcycle accident in 2004. As a firefighter, Jeff is no stranger to tragic accidents or shock and trauma. But nothing he's ever witnessed in the line of duty could have possibly prepared him for the death of his own child.

On the day of Jeffrey's accident, Jeff got a call from the hospital. The person on the other end of the line related what happened, and when Jeff asked how his son was doing, the response was, "We can't tell you that, but we can tell you it was a serious accident."

I stand corrected. This was the one thing being a firefighter had done to prepare Jeff for the unthinkable, because at that point he knew what the hospital was really trying to tell him. He knew it was code for the fact that Jeffrey was dead.

Jeff's son left behind a son of his own, and when he died, Jeff lost one of his best friends. Jeffrey was very athletic and did things to extremes. When he did something, he did it to the maximum.

"Jeffrey did everything I did, but better," Jeff says.

Before the accident, Jeff had been well known as a "life of the party" kind of guy. Cookouts, bonfires, camping, boating, or just about anything else that was good fun with good friends was part of Jeff's everyday life.

Now, not so much. He has become angry at people and he doesn't want to be that guy, but he understands he's not so much fun to be around anymore.

Because of all that, his friends don't often invite Jeff to events. Some of them make excuses when Jeff finds out after the fact, saying things like, "It just kind of came up spontaneously."

"It's okay, I get it," Jeff tells them. "You wanted to drink, have fun, make jokes, and laugh. Do all the things I used to do but can't anymore."

Without the drinking buddies he used to party with to hold him up in his grief, Jeff often comes home from work and has two or three drinks — too much, he says, but it helps him to cope — even if he knows it isn't all the best thinking. His wife is his best friend and he finds comfort in spending time with her, because she understands.

Life for Jeff in the aftermath of his son's death has become overwhelming. He can't do social stuff anymore, and although he often feels he's going in the wrong direction, he also feels there isn't a lot he can do about it. He's tried to hold onto his lifestyle, but the pressure of his grief is getting to him and it's making him tired. Plenty of the people in Jeff's life can see all of this, and as a result, some have recommended that he go and see a counselor.

But he's having none of that.

"Just because you have a piece of paper, it doesn't make you qualified to talk to me about the loss of a child," Jeff told me. "If there is nothing in your background that makes you qualified to help me, I don't want to hear it."

Over time, Jeff has regressed to the point where he wanted to find a source of real help that didn't require any trips to see a shrink, any explanations to satisfy inquiring minds, or any guilty feelings over the way he's responding to the death of his son. He found such a source in a place that not many grieving dads have spoken about in my discussions thus far.

He found it with animals.

Jeff lives in a small town and has enough acreage to escape his pain by spending time with his horses and his dogs. Sometimes, he goes camping for days at a time, choosing to capture some solace through a little quiet time with breathing creatures that don't ask questions or have complicated expectations. Instead, a pat on the head, a belly rub, and a little food every once in a while is all it takes.

Plus, he never has to explain himself to his horses or his dogs. They forgive him for everything, even when he's in a shitty mood. To Jeff's way of thinking, there's nothing more honest than an animal.

Jeff's son had a dog of his own, and Jeff has taken up care of the animal since Jeffrey can no longer do it. In fact, both of Jeff's dogs were lying at his feet while we conducted our interview in a hotel lobby. Taking care of Jeffrey's dog has been a real source of therapy for Jeff and his wife, because Jeffrey's dog seems to have a built-in sense of the times Jeff needs him most. Sometimes, Jeff and his wife will find themselves crying it out, and all of a sudden, Jeffrey's dog will come sauntering in to sit between them. Because of episodes like that, Jeff and his wife have come to believe that Jeffrey is living through the dog in some ways.

That sounds like real help to me — even if it didn't come from a support group or from a couch that's perched in a psychiatrist's office. And if you'll indulge me for a second, I hope you'll come to see that this kind of thinking is really the whole point of the "real help" concept.

You see, I don't really care whether a grieving dad gets what he needs from the pages of a book, from a counselor who's got a dozen degrees framed on his wall, or from a dog. In my opinion, grieving dads can get a little bit of "real help" from a lot of different places. In fact, getting all the help a grieving dad will ultimately need in just one place is clearly the exception, not the rule. And for those dads who have chosen to go the more common route that includes things like support groups, they often find (as I did) that it's not necessarily the support group itself that offers relief. Maybe, instead, the people we meet at the support group are the ones who provide real help.

Here's a bit of a key takeaway for you. When a grieving dad reaches outside his regular community of family and friends — when he turns to complete strangers, counselors, or support groups for real help — something funny winds up happening in the end.

Those people don't stay strangers for very long.

CHAPTER 7

BEYOND
THE HERE AND NOW

IN MY INTERVIEWS with grieving dads, I have discovered that we share quite a few "constants." These constants take on a variety of forms, but perhaps the most reliable constant I've encountered is this: we all ask questions about faith.

From Christians, Buddhists, and Muslims, to fathers of Hindu and Jewish faith, I've talked with people of just about every faith tradition there is — including self-proclaimed atheists and agnostics. Even the declared atheists have conformed to this constant I've mentioned, finding themselves asking questions of faith or a higher meaning.

Is there an afterlife?

Where is my child now?

Can my child communicate to me through dreams? Through animals? Through "pennies from heaven"?

Many of the grieving dads I've spoken with have experienced phenomenon related to questions like these. I call them questions from "beyond the here and now," because they reflect our natural desire as humans and as fathers to understand things outside the realities of our physical lives.

And of course, we'd like that same understanding to apply to the realities of our children's deaths.

Now, at this point, I'd like to make something clear. Lest you think this chapter is going to be all about attending church every Sunday, joining a Bible study group, or the "better place" where your child is now, I have some news. It's not about any of those things. Rather, this chapter is about experiences grieving dads like myself have had — experiences that might shed some light on the kinds of constants very few of us understand.

Hopefully, through examination of such experiences, we can all find ourselves just a step or two closer to some kind of meaning and understanding in the aftermath of tragic, life- shattering circumstances.

With that in mind, I'll begin with Angelo's story. Angelo happens to be the very first grieving dad I interviewed for this book, so I was a little nervous about some of the questions I was planning to ask him.

We met at a restaurant not far from where he lives, and just 33 seconds into our discussion, he took a call from a prospective employer. Yes, despite the fact that he lost his daughter over ten years ago to a random accident, Angelo was looking for a job on the day I met him.

His cordial tone and thoughtful answers betray his worldly need to earn money and provide for his family, whatever may be left of it in the wake of what happened to Celeste.

Celeste.

A beautiful, bright, and unsuspecting 17-year-old. Like most teenagers, she suffered from the illusion that she was indestructible. So, on an otherwise unremarkable day in 1999, she fell off the back of a moving mini-van while messing around with her friends.

Everything that happened afterwards is the reason Angelo and I got together to talk.

He recounts the story of the days he spent in the hospital with his wife, Laura. The hours slipped by as Angelo watched his daughter lying motionless in an intensive care bed. There were doctors, nurses, specialists, machines, and IV tubes everywhere. And there was trauma to Celeste's head.

The prognosis was not good.

First, there was talk of shaving off just a tiny part of Celeste's brain. As terrible as that sounded, it offered Angelo some hope. True, she'd have to relearn all the most fundamental things about living, but at the very least she'd be *alive.*

As time marched on, the "shave" idea morphed into something even more terrifying. After the doctors reviewed the MRI images and x-rays several more times, expectations for a "shave" yielding any positive results disappeared. Next, they were talking to Angelo and Laura about the horrible idea of taking a full *third* of her brain.

A third of her brain? What will become of Celeste if they take a third of her brain away?

Will she be able to dance?

Will she be able to smile?

Will she be able to acknowledge laughter, hate, or anger?

Will she even know it if we are in the same room with her?

These questions came to Angelo's mind. The answer to all of them was simple and clear.

No.

When this latest news was delivered and all encouraging prospects for Celeste seemed lost, Angelo walked away from the doctors, and found a corner in the hospital where he dropped to his knees and sobbed.

Shortly after that, a representative from the Gift of Hope organization walked into the room where Angelo was sitting with his wife, Laura. Angelo knew what this visit would mean. It would mean that he and Laura would be asked to give pieces of Celeste to strangers. And while Angelo could allow for the idea that those strangers deserved a chance at life, why wasn't the same true when it came to Celeste?

But for Celeste, there would be no miracle.

I asked Angelo if that made him feel abandoned by God.

"No, I didn't feel *abandoned* by God," he says. "I hated Him. Not just for me, but for my daughter. I asked Him, 'Where were you when she *needed* you?'"

Over time, Angelo came to ask himself, "What makes us so special that God would step in and change things, even in the face of so many kids who die every day?"

Today, however, Angelo has changed his views about God. While he can't say his faith is stronger, he can say his *life* is stronger, and that he has different expectations of God, even if he is more than a little put off about His plan for Celeste.

Angelo believes, but he won't ask God to help him to find a job. He has come to recognize that God doesn't work like a genie in a bottle, granting wishes for things like winning lottery tickets or gainful employment.

And as Angelo knows all too well, God doesn't rescue kids who fall off the back of moving mini-vans.

Looking back on those turbulent days in the hospital after Celeste's accident, Angelo remembers a cleaning lady and a male orderly who both worked in intensive care. They had repeatedly been in and out of Celeste's room, and they had both gone on about their business without Angelo exchanging so much as a word with either of them.

One day, as Angelo was in the hall crying, the cleaning lady came up to him and placed her hand on his shoulder.

"How is la niña?" the lady asked.

Angelo couldn't believe she was asking him this. Did she think he was out there in the hall crying tears of joy? Didn't she understand that his little girl was *dying*? After Angelo told her that things were not going well for la niña, the cleaning lady expressed her sympathy and promised to pray for Celeste.

Five minutes later, the male orderly did the same thing. Hand on the shoulder. Questions about how his daughter was doing. The same answers. The same promises about prayers.

This interaction with the cleaning lady and the male orderly went on for the week Celeste was in intensive care.

Today, even though Angelo wishes the outcome for Celeste were different, he now sees the possibility that God was there all along in people like the cleaning lady and the orderly. Somehow, those two people had the courage to approach a man who was leaning against a wall, sobbing uncontrollably, and lend him a hand of support.

"If God wasn't behind that, then who?" asks Angelo.

So, on a Friday in November of 1999, with the support of cleaning ladies and male orderlies, her doctors, the hospital staff, the people at Gift of Hope, and family, Celeste went away peacefully at the tender age of 17.

Because of the Gift of Hope organization, however, part of Celeste hasn't gone away at all. Now, Celeste is an organ donor.

Not "was." Is.

Her liver was given to a 3-year-old boy. One kidney went to a mother of four children. Her other kidney, her pancreas, and her leg bones, among other tissues, are all living within organ recipients fortunate enough to benefit from Celeste's generosity.

One such person, a woman who received Celeste's corneas, contacted Angelo through an intermediary. She wasn't able to reach out personally, but she wanted to let Angelo know that his family remains in her thoughts and prayers.

The man who received Celeste's pancreas, along with one of her kidneys, passed along a letter conveying his deep gratitude for her gift. Now, thanks to Celeste, he no longer has to endure dialysis and he is living a normal life once again with his wife and children.

For Angelo, the ultimate goal is to meet some of these recipients. No, he doesn't want to listen to Celeste's heart or feel her kidney through the skin of a stranger. He just wants to meet them, if for no other reason than to verify that the recipient realizes the tremendous gift Celeste has given. That, and the hope he can get a good sense the recipients are doing well and of course, that they are being good stewards of these incredible gifts from Celeste.

In the early months after his daughter's death, Angelo didn't think a whole lot about the people who received Celeste's gifts. He wasn't quite to that point just yet. Some days, he would cry as he stared out the window of his office at work. The window faced the Illinois State Police Forensic Lab, and strangely, Angelo would snap out of his despondency whenever he saw one particular state trooper come to work in the morning.

That state trooper would get out of his white van and walk into the building, and somehow seeing him do this simple morning routine would snap Angelo out of the spell his grief had cast upon him.

This went on for close to a year, until one day at a grieving parents meeting, this same state trooper walked in the door. He too had lost a daughter, maybe four months prior to showing up with his wife at the meeting.

So this, Angelo learned, was something he had in common with this officer. He took the time to tell the officer about the strange way that seeing the morning ritual of disembarking from the white van and coming into the building had somehow been a help to him.

Now he knows why.

Ultimately, Angelo and the state trooper became friends, and they shared their sad connection for some time before the trooper and his wife moved on to another city.

Other people in Angelo's life who he *thought* had moved on sometimes made new appearances. He tells me the story of a former co-worker, a younger woman he worked with for a few weeks in his past. She was a nice person, and Angelo liked her. When she left his company after just a few weeks, he had all but forgotten about her until one day, out of the blue, she shows up at the bereaved parents meeting Angelo was attending.

"Julie, what are *you* doing here?" Angelo asks.

It turns out she is there because her four-year-old boy died of an accidental hanging from a set of window blinds.

Window blinds. Seemingly such harmless devices, with a simple and innocent purpose, yet so suddenly and unceremoniously they take the life of an innocent four-year-old boy.

Julie, for her part, is totally devastated.

To this, Angelo can relate. The death of Celeste has alternately devastated, angered, debilitated, and crushed him in any number of ways the human mind might imagine. The bereaved parents meetings help, if only a little, but every once in a while the true nature of life's uncertainties strikes him hard. Like it does with the addition of Julie to the group. Like it does every time a new parent shows up at a meeting and tells a new story about how easy it is to be happy in your family life one moment, and facing the death of a child the next.

Julie and Angelo had lunch together on the same day I met with him. They do that sometimes, because now they have this unthinkable thing in common. This thing they can talk about together in a way that people who *haven't* lost a child cannot.

At lunch, Julie shows Angelo a tattoo. Julie feels comfortable sharing it because Angelo has a tattoo of his own on his arm. So, for half an hour, they talk about tattoos. For Julie, there is meaning in that discussion, since Angelo "gets it" that the tattoo is important to her. She appreciates the fact that Angelo will not judge her for it.

To Angelo, this half-hour discussion is more like a secret language they have between them, a language that no one else can speak or understand.

Tattoos. Window blinds. Random accidents.

Talking about those things in their conventional contexts would mean little to the average person. To a grieving dad, they take on a significance that is altogether different in a crazy, beyond the here and now sort of way.

"When my daughter died I did a lot of crazy things," Angelo says. "No sex binge or drugs or alcohol. But I went to a shaman, a medicine doctor, because I wanted to know my daughter was okay."

That visit cost Angelo a lot of money, but he didn't care. He also went to see two different mediums, just to do anything he could to connect with the daughter he loved, even if he knew all too well that she wasn't coming back.

Angelo tried Zoloft for a while, and fortunately pulled himself away from its soothing comfort in time to avoid any hint of dependency. He went to counselors, although he jokingly says, "I think I helped them more than they helped me. They had no street cred. You don't know, so don't try to act like you do."

Nonetheless, Angelo sees the value in counseling. "If one counselor doesn't work," he says, "go find another one. Don't give up."

Some of the "less conventional" things Angelo did, his wife knew about. Others she didn't. He just didn't feel obligated to obtain her stamp of approval, even though he never loved Laura any less. Still, they grew apart for a while, not because they didn't love each other, but because as is the case for so many grieving couples, the same incident induced different responses between the two of them.

"The second year after my daughter's death, I had *had* it," Angelo continues. "I'd had it with God, I'd had it with the world, I'd had it with everything. Enough is enough, I want her back, this is just a dream, and I wanna wake up."

But as Angelo and the rest of us grieving fathers know all too well, there is no waking up from this particular nightmare. As we sat there discussing that reality, the subject of suicide came up. I asked Angelo point-blank whether or not it was something he'd ever considered. "I don't know what I would do," he told me. "I wasn't brave enough to put a bullet in my head, but I may have been brave enough to swallow a whole bottle of pills."

Sobering thought. After hearing his honest response, I prompted Angelo for less morbid reflections, and he began thinking about the time in his life when Celeste was 16. He remembers planning a trip to Italy with Laura to celebrate their twentieth wedding anniversary, which was to be a romantic getaway for just the two of them. But as he reflected upon how much he loved being a father, he told Laura that they should take the kids (they have a second daughter, Celeste's younger sister, Beth) with them.

"Celeste won't be with us much longer," he remembers saying. He meant, of course, that as a 16-year-old she would soon go away to college and get married like kids are supposed to do. He could not have known that his words would ultimately be so prophetic in such a different way, but those words haunt him to this very day just the same.

Thankfully, Celeste and Beth did indeed join their parents on that trip. They had a wonderful time as a family on that vacation, and Angelo remains grateful that they spent it together. Never mind that he may wish Celeste could be back in Italy today, perhaps enjoying her honeymoon like others in her age group might be doing right now.

In the end, Angelo doesn't know what helped him through all of this. "Perseverance, maybe," he offers. However, he has come to recognize that God might have been there for him and for Celeste all along. He was there in the people all around Angelo, his family, and the compassionate strangers he met throughout this journey.

Perhaps that alone is a big part of what helps him to heal, but he's pretty sure it wasn't the shaman or the counselors that made the difference. For Angelo, there is another kind of therapy that works better than anything else — talking about Celeste.

Where have we heard that before? Only from every grieving dad I've talked to, of course. All of the grieving fathers I've interviewed have told me that just as Angelo said, there is meaning and understanding in talking about the children that left this life too early.

It's another constant.

It's been a constant for me, I can tell you. And I can also tell you that knowing others in my situation feel the same brings me some comfort. Not that I want them to feel the pain — but knowing I am not alone has helped me tremendously.

Another dad who feels the same — and has the credentials to bring some authority to this kind of thinking — is Charlie, who is a grieving dad with a Ph.D. in philosophy, two facts that bring him some unique perspectives. Not just about the therapeutic benefits of talking about one's deceased child, but also about things that fall into the "beyond the here and now" category.

Charlie and I spent a beautiful summer afternoon on his patio overlooking the flower garden he created for his daughter, Heidi. We talked about many different things regarding the experiences with our losses, including the creation of memorial gardens. Charlie taught me a little about planting forget-me-not flowers that day, because I noticed a lot of them in his backyard. In fact, I plant the pink and blue variety every year for Katie and Noah.

Charlie's daughter, Heidi, died at the age of 21 due to complications with leukemia. Since her death in 2003, Charlie has had plenty of time to put his study of philosophy to work. Not that it always helps — particularly when it came to his relationships at work.

Charlie spent the bulk of his career as an accomplished professor and Dean of Continuing Studies at the Catholic college where he worked. After Heidi passed away, Charlie felt that his co-workers didn't support him as much as he would have thought — especially given the Christian values their school was sworn to uphold. In fact, not even the campus priest reached out to him.

This was difficult for Charlie to swallow, since he felt he'd always been there for his co-workers in the past. Still, he overcame the disappointment he felt, choosing to seek support from other places.

"Grieving is all about attitude," Charlie told me during our interview. "An important part of healing is to recognize that fact."

Charlie recognizes that fact, for sure. His attitude regarding grief has been shaped not only by his doctorate in philosophy, but also by his experiences since Heidi died. He believes that grieving dads have to "ride the wave of grief" on its terms; in other words, we don't get to pick and choose the conditions of how the pain of losing a child will be navigated.

"You can't fight it," Charlie says. "Let it be what it is. You are not in charge. You can't fix it." In addition to all that, Charlie also advises grieving dads to avoid asking the question, "Why?"

Why should we avoid that question? "It's unhealthy thinking," he responds. "Because there are no answers."

What, then, is "healthy" thinking when it comes to pondering the death of a child? From Charlie's perspective, there are several things to consider in that regard. First, he believes that grieving dads should surround themselves with other grieving dads and parents. "There is comfort in being around others that get it," he told me. He also suggests that at a minimum, it makes sense to "surround yourself with compassionate people."

Preferably, the kind that will cry right along with you. Or at least, the kind that can avoid the urge to run away if they catch a tear running down your cheek.

With regard to religion, as applied to this whole "beyond the here and now" thing, Charlie advises caution. He knows people turn to churches for help, but the problem is that churches are made up of people. "People do and say stupid things, regardless if they're in church or not," Charlie warns. Pretty sound advice, coming from a Lutheran deacon. I can relate to this advice. For his part, Charlie's spirituality has more positively influenced his healing than his religion.

Speaking of which, Charlie believes that he has received spiritual "signs" from his daughter. For example, shortly after Heidi died, he recalls a day where a hummingbird followed him around his backyard for about 15 minutes. I'm no hummingbird expert, but in my experience, hummingbirds don't stay in one place longer than a few seconds, do they?

Charlie and his wife also believe they have been blessed with the phenomenon of "pennies from heaven." If you're not familiar, the concept refers to the mysterious appearance of coins (or sometimes feathers) with an uncanny sense of timing. In my own case, I have had pennies show up at strange times in strange places when I'm thinking about Katie. When Noah is on my mind, it's dimes. Sometimes I find them together, but rarely do I find other coins. I thought I was alone in this until I started interviewing other dads for this book. All of this is sort of hard to explain, but a surprising number of grieving dads have told me similar stories. And you don't have to take my word for it; google "pennies from heaven and grief," and you'll see what I mean.

Whether it's pennies from heaven, hummingbirds, or any other sign that comes to us from our children, Charlie believes very much in the spiritual side of grieving. It's just as important, he told me, as the physical or the psychological aspects of a father's grief. "All three go hand in hand," Charlie asserts.

I couldn't agree more.

Charlie also feels strongly that it's important for grieving dads to do their best to forgive people that can't be there for us. In his view, they don't understand or have the capacity to comprehend the experience of losing a child. In fact, just about everything Charlie had to say during our interview was thought provoking and inspirational, but perhaps his best advice was this: grieving dads need to get beyond the "should have" life.

"Mow or don't mow," he told me. "Pull weeds or don't pull weeds." Either "do" or "don't do" are better choices, Charlie says, than moping around and muttering about what you "should" be doing.

Once again, Charlie, I couldn't agree more. All too often in life, the "doing" part of anything is the hardest. The same is true with regard to grief. This I know from firsthand experience, because it wasn't until I made a pact with myself to "do" the grief — in other words, to actually embrace and acknowledge it — before I really started the long, slow process of healing.

Please don't let the word "slow" scare you, but I can tell you that many times in my journey through the deaths of my children, I have had to remind myself that healing simply doesn't happen overnight. Like most men, I'm a solution-oriented kind of guy; if there is a problem, I'd rather *solve* it than sit around talking about it. Unfortunately, I learned the hard way that this *problem* has no solution or cure.

And that's the thing. *Nothing* cures grief. It can only be controlled, or managed — but it can never be "cured." Once I caught on to that little riddle, it helped me to begin to manage my own grief and kick-start the healing process — or at least get it moving in the right direction.

When it comes to the quest for meaning and understanding, one grieving dad I interviewed had an interesting approach. His name is Phil.

I met Phil in my home state of Iowa, during a bicycle-enthusiasts event called RAGBRAI, which stands for the Register's Annual Great Bicycle Ride Across Iowa. It's a seven-day event that's been around for 40 years now, and as such, it's the largest, oldest bicycle touring event in the world. It's also the longest.

I think that's the part Phil likes best.

After our extended day of riding, Phil and I met up and shared a few beers. During my interview with him, Phil revealed to me that he had ridden his bike 8,000 miles the year I met with him. Eight thousand miles! To put that into some perspective, pretend for a moment that the custodians of our tax dollars in Washington decided we needed to build a bike trail from Honolulu, Hawaii to St. Louis, Missouri. Phil would have to climb on his bike and ride the path from St. Louis to Honolulu — then turn around and go *back* to St. Louis on the same path — before he'd be able to log 8,000 miles. (For the record, such a trip would still leave him about 200 miles short.)

Obviously, Phil is a serious rider. One of the things I found interesting about him is the fact that he was making the RAGBRAI trip by himself, having traveled all the way from his hometown in the state of Washington to be at the event.

For Phil, long bike rides had been an integral part of his life even before his son, Andrew, passed away in 2002. His death happened at home, because Andrew, who was a successful baseball player in high school, had the misfortune of being born with an enlarged heart. Phil and his wife found him in bed. He was only 19.

The "athlete" part of Andrew was a major point of attachment between father and son. In fact, Phil and Andrew bicycled across the United States together.

Twice.

"Riding is beyond passion," Phil told me. "It's strong therapy. It's become a sick obsession, but I feel more connected with him when I ride."

After Andrew died, it took Phil a while to grasp hold of the idea that riding his bike could provide a unique connection back to his son. In fact, he couldn't even force himself to get back on his bicycle for almost a month after his son's passing. He had neither the desire nor the energy.

"I almost forgot how to ride a bike," Phil says. "I had lost confidence in a lot of my abilities." I hear this a lot from grieving dads, and I've experienced it myself.

Somehow, Phil eventually gathered the strength to ride, and it's become his central way of getting beyond what is here and now in his life. On several occasions, Phil has attended international cycling events, some of which occur in third world countries. "People ask me, 'Aren't you afraid?'" Phil says of such adventures: "I tell them, no, my kid has died. Nothing can happen to me. The worst has already happened."

Phil would like to rejoin society, but that thought competes with darker ones. He told me the day we met that he'd recently said to a friend that he "didn't care" anymore. Worse, he said, "I don't even care that I don't care."

As Phil and the rest of the grieving dads I've interviewed know all too well, the domain of the grieving dad is a lonely place. Men, in general, have a tendency to isolate, and the death of a child can bring about this affinity in a magnified way. The ironic part is that it doesn't have to be that way. We really just need to find other grieving dads to be with. Believe me, there are a lot of us out there to connect with — we just need to make the effort to find each other — even if it's just someone you can grab a coffee or beer with from time to time. Hell, you don't even have to talk about your losses. But whether you're talking or not, there is a sense of peace just being around another dad that gets what you have been through, and will be there for you on days that are not going so well.

Phil already recognized this philosophy shortly before the time we met. Nevertheless, for the foreseeable future, Phil intends to find his way beyond the here and now through cycling. It brings him closer to his son, and for the time being, it seems to work best.

Ride on then, Phil. Ride on.

To me, bicycling is part of my fitness program, and so is running. These are pastimes that help to keep me in shape. They also help me to burn off energy, and yes, they help to burn off some anxiety and anger, too. So although I don't personally connect with my own deceased children through riding or running, I can see how these things can help.

For a look at another "beyond the here and now" kind of connection, we'll turn again to Ed from chapter three. My interview with Ed was one of the most remarkable interviews I conducted. His candor and the intensity of his feelings really came through when we talked, and I found our discussion to be a profoundly interesting experience.

Ed's son, Jesse, died in single car accident late in 2009. Jesse was by himself in the truck, having dropped a group of friends off after a day of fishing. The reason for the accident is unclear, but some have speculated that perhaps Jesse swerved off the road to avoid a deer. Whatever the reason behind the accident, Jesse was ejected from the car, and he died instantly at the scene.

Afterwards, in another example of the cruel parade of constants grieving dads have to face, Ed went through all the customary emotional upheavals. He fights depression, anxiety attacks, memory loss, uncontrollable sobbing, and worse. When it all got to be too much, he even considered suicide.

"I won't lie to you," Ed reflected. "First three months, I came very close to swallowing a gun."

Understandable, under the circumstance. Jesse was Ed's best friend, and when he passed away, Ed's life changed forever.

One more constant.

Still, Ed is very grateful for the 23 years that he shared with his son. Sometimes, he looks for a renewed connection with Jesse through his son's guitar. He grabs it, goes upstairs, shuts the door and plays while he cries. It's his therapy. But it isn't his *only* therapy.

To put it bluntly, Ed believes that Jesse himself has provided a bit of therapy as well. He's done it from beyond the here and now, and he's done it twice, according to Ed.

The first time, Ed was working by himself in a rock quarry (Ed is a heavy equipment operator) when he got dangerously close to a huge drop-off on very loose rock. All of a sudden, a butterfly came out of nowhere in the bottom of this quarry and landed on Ed's windshield. Then, it flew off, backed up, and hit the windshield — not once, but several times in a row.

"I finally got the hint and backed the machine away from the edge," Ed told me. "Then the butterfly left." Ed believes his son was responsible and was looking out for him that day.

Ed's second otherworldly encounter with Jesse happened during a dream. In the dream, Ed saw Jesse driving a truck going down a country road at night. Jesse wasn't wearing a seatbelt in the dream (for the record, he wasn't on the night of his accident, either). No seatbelt, despite cruising along at 70-80 miles an hour — so in the dream, Ed told his son to slow down.

"He looked at me and said, 'I'll be okay, Dad. I'll be okay,'" Ed remembers.

As the dream continued, the truck started to skid sideways and went into a roll. Ed found himself hovering above the truck watching all of this unfold — and then he woke up. When he did, there was no hint of the tremors or tears that would normally accompany this type of nightmare.

That's because to Ed, it wasn't a nightmare at all. "It's like he was telling me he was okay," Ed reflected.

I wasn't there in that dream with Ed, but let me tell you something. There was such conviction in Ed's voice that I couldn't help but think he was relating matters of fact, rather than a symbolic story about a fairytale dream.

You see, one of the many things I've learned from my discussions with grieving dads is that encounters from beyond the here and now are far more common than one would guess. Further, whether you're an atheist, an agnostic, or a believer, there's another constant to be observed. That is, the death of a child sends all of us to our knees. Not necessarily in prayer. But at the very least, in a deep yearning for answers to some very difficult questions indeed.

CHAPTER 8

THE LONG VIEW

Don't LET THE word "long" scare you away, because if you stay with me a minute, you'll see there is reason for hope.

As I mentioned in the last chapter, the realities a grieving dad faces are full of constants. One of the more unsettling ones is the fact that there will never be a day when we are *not* in mourning for the children who left us behind.

But there is another side to that particular constant. It's a hard one to grasp, especially for a newly bereaved father — but believe it or not, things *will* eventually get better. I wish I could tell you when, but I can't. And believe it or not, in my talks with grieving dads from all corners of the planet, this is a constant — an invaluable message, really — that fathers whose children died years ago can offer to those who are only beginning their journey through grief.

I know it sounds crazy. I mean, I *know,* because I thought the very same things when Katie and Noah passed away. I thought things would *never* get better. I thought I would surely die before I could ever hope to live something close to a normal life again. Of course, "normal" is a relative thing in this particular context. We can never really go back to the "normal" we were before the death of our children. How could we? But you will come to learn that it's possible to find a *new* normal. It took me a while to realize this, because I spent a lot of time and energy trying to get back to my old normal rather than focusing on establishing a new one.

More on "normal" in chapter ten. For now, I'll say it once more. There will never be a day when a grieving father isn't in mourning. But with the passage of time, I promise you the pain recedes. It diminishes slowly, but it does start to fade — in small, yet measurable doses. Remnants of our experiences will always be a part of us, but the waves of grief start to pull back ever so slowly.

In this chapter, we will explore this constant through the experiences of three grieving dads I interviewed. The first of them is Jon, whom you met briefly in chapter three. Unfortunately, Jon is an especially seasoned grieving dad. He and his wife, Linda, have faced the death of a child on three separate occasions.

The first loss happened in 1972. Against his better judgment (and that of his wife's physician), Jon and Linda made a trip by airplane early in the third trimester of pregnancy. "She was seven months pregnant and the doctor advised against the trip," Jon says. "I knew more than the doctor."

The morning after returning home from the ill-advised trip, Linda's water broke a full two months before she was due to give birth. Jon rushed her to the hospital, where Linda endured a long, hard labor before finally delivering the couple's son at midnight the following day.

They named him Little Jon.

Big Jon was blissfully ignorant of his tiny son's precarious situation. The nurses, however, were not. They rushed the little boy to the nursery, putting him in an incubator with oxygen. Still, Jon was proud of his son and spent a lot of time admiring him through the nursery window, convinced that Little Jon would pull through.

"I was proud as a peacock," Jon recalls.

Linda, on the other hand, was in and out of drug-induced sleep in the early hours since Little Jon's birth. She made it out of bed to see her son in the nursery just once. Sometime around mid-morning, a doctor visited Jon and Linda, and told them Little Jon suffered from hyaline membrane syndrome. The disease is common among premature babies, and it affects the respiratory system by lining the air sacs in the lungs with a membrane composed of proteins and dead cells.

Little Jon was indeed suffering from this affliction, but the physician offered a ray of hope nonetheless. In his view, the baby was doing a bit better than when he was first brought to the incubator. After the visit from the doctor, Jon returned to his post outside the nursery window. At this point, the danger his son was facing seemed more apparent than ever; Little Jon's chest was laboring, heaving up and down with each feeble attempt to take in just a little air.

Back and forth Jon went, between the nursery and his wife's hospital room, checking in on Linda and Little Jon as best he could. During one of the trips to the nursery, Jon was informed that a Lutheran nurse had baptized Little Jon. During another, Jon arrived at the window just in time to see a different nurse rolling his son's incubator away. Inside, Little Jon's body was no longer laboring to breath.

After fighting the good fight for about 13 hours, Little Jon passed away.

Jon turned from the nursery window in denial. "That wasn't my son that I saw," he remembers thinking. "He must have been someone else's." But just a few minutes later, the worst was confirmed when another nurse tracked Jon down to give him the bad news.

"I walked to Linda's room, bent over her, and said, 'It's over.'" She knew what Jon meant.

Afterwards, the couple had a long and quiet trip back home, during which neither of them could think of much to say. The same was true in the following days, as the realization sunk in that their lives were forever changed. "It was as if someone had ripped our hearts out," Jon indicated.

"One day at work," he continued, "I felt the emotions swelling up in me, so I went to speak with one of the pastors I worked with. I told him that I couldn't cry in front of Linda. I had to be strong for her." The pastor had a simple, one-word response.

"Why?"

So Jon went home and had a very good cry with Linda. And as Jon says today, real men cry. "If Jesus can show grief," he reasons, "why can't we? Men don't need anyone's permission to grieve."

That advice would serve Jon as well as it could — two more times. Throughout the early '70s, Jon and Linda tried for another baby. Finally, she became pregnant again, but a miscarriage dashed the couple's hopes early in the first trimester. Another miscarriage, which occurred after Linda got the flu, happened during her third pregnancy.

Jon remembers asking, "How could God allow this to happen to us?" He also remembers turning away from God for a period of time during this phase of his life. This was very unusual for Jon, because he had always enjoyed "a close relationship with God for most of my life."

Of course, the death of a child can change all that. The death of *three* children can change it for good.

Linda, however, never wavered in her faith. She attended Sunday services without fail, even while Jon took a leave of absence, preferring to read the newspaper in a local restaurant instead.

This, it seems, is a normal reaction for many grieving dads. I won't call it another constant, because for just as many grieving dads, dedication to a life with God remains just as it did for Linda. A constant in and of itself — and one that not only never flickers, but sometimes becomes even stronger than before the death of a child.

Remember, everyone is different. And "normal" is different after the death of a child, too.

Over time, Jon began to wonder when Linda and he would enjoy life again. "With such death," he says, "there is often a feeling of guilt that accompanies anything representing enjoyment."

The same was true regarding the couple's renewed attempts to start a family. There were more tests. There were more tears. And through it all, despite the short adjournment from Sunday services that Jon undertook, there was prayer.

At last, the couple became pregnant for the fourth time early in 1976. With the passing of each uneventful month, cautious optimism slowly gave way to real hope. Then, in December of 1976, Jon and Linda's dreams finally came true. Their son, Brian, a healthy little baby boy, was born. There would be more tears — but this time, they would be tears of joy.

The couple would experience that joy again in 1981, when their daughter, Jessica, would come into their lives. Finally, the family was complete — even if the memories of Little Jon and the couple's two miscarriages would never go away completely.

For a long time after Little Jon's death, Jon Sr. blamed himself. Even when the shock and trauma eventually subsided, guilt and remorse took their place. Which sort of reminds me of something we touched on earlier in this book.

Something to do with carrying heavy loads.

"Guilt is a heavy burden," Jon reasons. "One which many parents of deceased children carry. It is much too heavy a load for us. We must find a way to rid ourselves of this weight."

Guilt is another constant I've heard about over and over amongst the grieving dads I interviewed for this book. As men, we are the protectors. If our child dies, we tell ourselves we failed as dads because we didn't protect our children. Guilt can be the great destroyer, and to be very honest, guilt is what almost destroyed me.

"I am very sensitive to what other grieving parents are experiencing," Jon continues. "The pain, the guilt, the anger. God has taken all this away from my heart, but I still have moments of remorse."

Jon's comments here are once again very similar to those of the overwhelming majority of grieving dads who've spoken with me. As I indicated at the beginning of this chapter, the moments of sadness and remorse will never entirely go away. They will always be there, even as they eventually shrink in size and frequency. But nevertheless, as Jon's message indicates, there is some relief to be gained from the pain diminishing over time.

Jon has picked up a few additional messages in his long-view reflections. First, he suggests that grieving dads should seek help from a counselor trained specifically for grief counseling. In Jon's view, that counselor would ideally be of the Christian persuasion. From my perspective, the truly important aspect is seeking the counsel in the first place. Either way, there is no guarantee that a member of any clergy will be adequately trained in the subject of grief. As such, be sure to clarify that point before diving in. If you find a counselor that doesn't work for you, look for one that has been through the death of a child and can relate on a personal level rather than what they learned in the classroom. Someone that has walked the walk.

Jon and his wife have taken that good advice. For the past five years, they have attended Compassionate Friends meetings. The meetings help, but from Jon's point of view, they are beneficial to him because he feels he can set aside his own grief for a while, and focus upon using his experiences to facilitate the healing of others.

"Be patient with yourself," Jon conveys in his comments. "I recently read that grief is a spiritual experience requiring a spiritual solution. In this lifetime, there is no resolution, merely assimilation. Resolution will come in the afterlife."

Jon also advises that grieving dads should take heed of the counsel his pastor offered, which was relatively simple. "Weep," Jon says. "It's okay to cry."

--

Clearly, a close relationship with God and continued observance of his religious beliefs have given Jon a "long view" approach to dealing with grief. But religion does not provide the only window to the long view. There are other ways to see the picture, and we can look through the eyes of Tony for a peek into what I mean.

Like Jon, Tony's experience as a grieving dad goes back a few years. His son, Randy, died in 1987 at the age of 21. Too young to die — but old enough to decide things for himself.

Including the terms of his own death.

"The day he died," Tony told me during my interview with him, "I was taking a vacation day. The phone rang very early in the morning. It was UPS — Randy's boss." Apparently, the boss was looking for Randy, who hadn't shown up for work.

"Show up for work?" Tony asked the boss. "We were awake when he left. We heard him." Nonetheless, after looking out of the front window of the house, Tony could see Randy's car sitting right there in the driveway. He went downstairs to look around — still no sign of Randy. In fact, his son's bed didn't look slept in, and his closet door was wide open.

This was not like Tony's son at all, so the alarm bells went off right away. Randy would never just leave his car in the driveway, because doing so would block his mother in. The couple became more thoroughly baffled as the minutes dragged on — especially when Tony's wife, Brenda, discovered her son's shotgun was missing.

Tony had purchased two guns for Randy's sixteenth birthday: a .22 caliber and a 12-gauge shotgun. He and Randy took gun safety courses and hunted together — this was kind of their thing — one of the ways they spent time together as father and son.

"His car is still here, the gun is gone," Tony continued. "Did he get pissed at someone? Is he chasing someone around with a gun?" These questions seemed natural at the time, fueled by the fact that they had always kept guns and ammo locked away separately. Thus, when Brenda saw the .22 caliber sitting out in the open, the couple knew something was very wrong.

As the situation became more troubling by the second, the couple called Randy's girlfriend to see if she could shed some light on their son's whereabouts. When the girlfriend confirmed the timeline that seemed to line up with Randy's arrival the previous evening, Tony finally gave in to his suspicions and called the police. "I said I don't think there's anything wrong, but I have a gun missing — I think — and I don't know where he is. I don't know why his car's here and he isn't," Tony recollects.

So the police put a report in the system.

Some time later, around 11:00 the same morning, an officer came to their front door. This seemed odd to Tony; how could a cop be at his front door, yet no police car be anywhere in sight? Once more, something didn't seem right, and the alarm bells began clanging in Tony's head all over again.

Anxious for an update about Randy, Tony's wife joined him at the door. "Did you find him?" she asked.

"Call the coroner, ma'am," came the response.

Brenda looked at Tony in terror, the realization sinking in immediately. One doesn't call a coroner unless there is a death. Their son's death, in this case.

Later, everything would become clearer. Tony surmises that Randy must have left the house with the gun, crossing through a neighbor's yard to a field nearby an elementary school. In that field, years ago, Randy and a neighborhood friend had built a fort. For whatever reason, that fort held an important place in Randy's heart — important enough to become the place where he would choose to die.

"We know now he went to his fort, opened his wallet to his driver's license, and shot himself," Tony tells me.

Looking back on the police response to the incident, Tony now says that it's provided a sense of purpose. "From that moment on, one of our missions is to play an advocate — if we could — between 'Call the coroner' and having sensitivity at the front door, without jeopardizing the crime scene."

Looking back on my interview with Tony, to this day I'm still shocked at the lack of compassion displayed by the officer who came to the door that day.

"Call the coroner." Really?

Unfortunately, this isn't the first time I've heard something similar to this. Nick, who we met earlier in this book, mentioned to me he was sitting on the front steps of his house when he overheard the EMT and police officer talking about how beautiful a day it was outside. "Here I was," Nick told me, "sitting on the front steps, trying to wrap my head around the fact they just carried my daughter out of the house and they were talking about the weather."

Lack of compassion, to say the least.

Back to Tony's story. In most states, a suicide is treated as a homicide until proven otherwise. Once murder is ruled out, it seems logical that the investigation should end. "You don't need to explain why the suicide occurred, other than [the fact] it wasn't a murder," Tony reasons.

It didn't take long to surmise the cause of Randy's death. And so began Tony's journey to forever.

Brenda wanted a funeral for her son, but Tony did not. He didn't want calling hours or services or a burial or anything else representing the finality of the situation.

"I was angry," Tony says. "I didn't want him dead. I didn't want to acknowledge the fact that if I buried him, that meant he would be dead." With this line of thinking, Tony tried to get Brenda to change her mind about a full-out funeral. He suggested to his wife that the couple could "do what we've got to do and get on with our lives."

Brenda said no. So Tony told her she would have to make the arrangements — which she did.

One thing during the process of planning the funeral that gave Brenda pause was the issue of choosing a casket. This isn't something anyone wants to do, and I remember all too well having to pick out urns for Katie and Noah. I can certainly sympathize with Brenda on this issue, and Tony felt the same. "Neither of us wanted to do that," he recalls.

Another moment of horror came for Tony when the funeral director tried to give him Randy's clothes — which despite the circumstances, were actually clean.

"I freaked," Tony told me. "I screamed, I remember myself screaming. [Brenda] said, 'just get rid of them.' Now I wish we hadn't."

Going to the memorial service, Tony was lost. He had given up, and with both he and his wife crying through the whole ordeal, he finally suggested that they simply go home. The couple stopped at several churches on the way, hoping to find a bereavement meeting. Someone finally steered them in the right direction, but it would be a month before they could finally attend a gathering. In the meantime, Tony would remain numb.

When they arrived at the support meeting, Tony could hear people laughing in the room, and he remembers thinking, "Maybe one day I'll be able to tell a joke."

A respected grief counselor was in attendance at the meeting. Tony walked up to him and asked a simple question: "Can I die of a broken heart?" The reply was simply:

"I suppose. It hurts that much."

At that moment, Tony came to realize the stark differences between compassionate people and those who speak before their brains are engaged. Illustrating his point, he says, "What happens in the beginning days, or whenever traumatic events happen, stays [with you] forever. The police at the door will always be at the door, and they'll always say, 'Call the coroner, ma'am.' The grief counselor will always be compassionate."

A long-view manner of thinking, for sure. To me, Tony's point is more evidence of how a grieving dad with long-term experience can provide support to a newly bereaved father to help him understand what he's facing.

Speaking of support, it seems that in the years since Randy's death, the quest for help and support has become a central focus for Tony and Brenda. The experience with the grief counselor led Tony to seek further outlets for the pain he was feeling. Consequently, he and his wife began attending Compassionate Friends and Bereaved Parents of the USA group meetings.

"Almost all of it — talking to people, going to group meetings — generates an energy within me that works. We've sat with people and cried with them. What works is going through it. You don't hide it," Tony says.

But sadly, many guys do try to hide it. "Some guys come back and say 'I can't revisit it, I don't want to go there,'" Tony tells me. "The real way through it *is* going there. Go there and scream about it, punch walls about it, cry about it, and get mad about it. When you start beating it up enough times, it gets planted in a place that's copasetic. When guys grieve, we're [usually] not guys that cry together. Although we could, and I've learned that we could. For men there were no major grief outlets. Bury your grief and move on."

In Tony's experience, with a bereavement meeting that has men in attendance, the opportunity for a guy-to-guy relationship to form becomes possible. To his way of thinking, such relationships could further evolve outside the circle. But when men and women are interacting at a group meeting, there is also the possibility that a man may say something to offend a woman in attendance.

Again, we simply grieve differently. To wit, sometimes just yelling, *"What the fuck!"* out loud can be a legitimate form of therapy to a grieving dad.

One thing that Tony has found to be fairly universal, regardless of gender, is blame. "With all the people we've met over the years, there's more people than not who blame themselves. If it's a miscarriage, Mom insists it's what she ate. In my case with suicide, I insisted I was just a damn bad dad. I'm a firm believer that in suicide, nobody dies wanting to die. They die wanting to escape their pain. If I can fall back to the pain when he died, yeah I wanted to die, too. I really wasn't ready to load a gun. But let me die — let this thing break my heart because I don't want to hurt anymore."

Instead of giving in to emotions like that one, Tony has found renewed strength over the years that come from a decidedly long-view state of mind. He hasn't stopped at simply attending group meetings at occasional intervals. Rather, he's become an advocate and regular speaker at local schools on the subject of suicide. Tony also makes himself available to other grieving dads in his community.

Just like Tony, I too do what I can to help others going through this pain. There is healing in helping others. Everyone knows the saying, "Misery loves company," but I think it should say, "Misery *needs* company." We cannot do this alone, nor should we expect ourselves to be able to. I believe that once we can stand on our own two feet, reaching out to help others will continue to assist with our own healing.

For an example of the power of advocacy, on one occasion, Tony found himself speaking in front of a group of young adults, retelling Randy's story for what had to be the thousandth time. He spoke for a couple of hours, and when he was finished, a female student followed him out of the venue. She told Tony that she had heard him speak the year before, and at the time, she was "in the same place that Randy was. I had so much work and so many expectations," she told Tony, "and everything was dumping on me. I felt like I was getting buried by the day. And then I heard you talk."

The next day, this girl called her counselor, who helped her to clear everything up. As a result of the way Tony had reached her through his talk, the girl told him she had "never been so happy" in all her life.

I asked Tony how that made him feel. "It makes me feel that Randy's talking. It makes me feel that I made an impact."

I was glad to hear Tony say that. It confirms my own conviction that a beneficial long view of grief usually includes finding ways to allow our children to speak through us. For those willing to embrace the idea that we can help others through the experiences of our children, the rewards are potentially great.

Taking such a long-view approach isn't always easy, of course. Simply having the desire to help others doesn't guarantee that the "others" will accept your help in the first place. Don't take my word for it; we'll have a look at the experiences of Joe for some insight to what I'm getting at here.

I had breakfast with Joe and his family, ironically enough, on Father's Day in 2010. Joe and I met as a result of his son, Jimmy, passing away after a horrific ATV accident. It happened when the boy was just 13 years old.

"We were up in the Rocky Mountains when it happened and that was the problem," Joe recalled. "We couldn't get him to the hospital. We tried CPR. The helicopter was circling overhead and the ambulance came roaring up. The helicopter carried the medics, and they didn't have anywhere to land. They had to go find a clearing and then run up. It was insane, just crazy."

At the time, Joe was divorced from Jimmy's mother, so the situation took on a few complexities. There was the typical "convincing" that a father will sometimes do with any mother — all of the "we'll be safe" stuff that accompanies a trip like the one Joe and Jimmy were taking together. Obviously, the promises to keep their son out of harm's way have haunted Joe, and to this day he remembers the phone call to his ex-wife as perhaps the most difficult five minutes of his life.

"That phone call, an hour after," Joe reflected. "I said, 'I don't know if I can make this call.' But I had to, that's my responsibility."

Later, when it was time to fly back home from the Denver airport, Joe remembers staring blankly out the window at the plane he was soon to board. "Something caught my eye," he told me. "They were loading my son's body onto the airplane. I'm standing there watching them load the casket with my son in it into the bottom of the airplane that I'm going to get on. That was a really difficult moment."

When their plane landed, Joe's ex-brother-in-law was there, and he's sure that Jimmy's uncle blamed Joe for what happened. "I took him on vacation and let him on an ATV that killed him. He was 13. [The ATV] was a full-sized one, and that was my mistake. I didn't do any research on them; there was a sticker on there: *Must be 16*. But he was a big kid. He couldn't wait to get home and tell his friends that he was up in the Rocky Mountains riding an ATV."

Remember what I said about guilt being a constant? Joe carries a lot of it around today, even if he's "come to grips with it," as he told me.

For a while after the accident, Joe may have considered trying to ease the guilt by finding another source of blame. As many grieving dads faced with similar situations, Joe briefly considered taking action against the ATV manufacturer. He dismissed the idea after thinking it through. "I can't go sit in front of a room full of strangers, have them point their finger at me and tell me it's my fault. If we get a million dollars, what is that going to change? Nothing's bringing my son back."

Nonetheless, Joe did embrace an advocacy stance about ATVs. "They market ATVs as family fun but there's an astonishing number of children that get maimed and killed on these. I was not in the mindset to do anything but my ex-wife's brother did all the research. He went in front of Congress. They changed some of the laws but not nationally. I don't know really whatever happened."

To Joe, things like lawsuits and advocacy groups aren't necessarily the stuff that a real long view about grief is made from. Instead, he holds on to more meaningful things — such as an amazingly clear dream he had about Jimmy one night.

"We were at the hockey rink and I was watching the hockey game of my buddy's kids," Joe told me. "In the hallway, kids were playing a game and I saw my buddy's sons. Then I turned around and there was Jimmy. I said, 'Jimmy, what are you doing?' He said, 'Dad, I'm going to be okay.' And then I woke up. I sat up in bed, tears were rolling down my face. A sign he's going to be okay. Every day you wake up and reality hits. It smacks you in the face, punches you in the stomach. That dream calmed me. Now he's taking care of me."

Our interview together was the first time Joe had ever shared the story of his dream about Jimmy. Hearing that made me feel pretty good about writing this book, because it reinforced the idea that grieving dads need other grieving dads to truly open up and face their situations head on.

I think Joe feels the same. And he's also felt the frustration of trying to get grieving dads to set their macho misgivings aside and seek the help they need. "I want to help people," he says. "But I'm searching for the way. I came up with the idea of a group for fathers. I'm frustrated I can't get anybody to show up. But I'm looking at other ways to get the word out. One guy showed up. He was just pouring his guts out. When he left, he said it was so nice to talk to somebody that understands."

I understand too, Joe. In all I've learned about the long view of grief, men *need* to grieve with other men who've been there themselves. There is simply no better way to develop a connection that is truly meaningful to a grieving dad. I have seen the power of this firsthand in the workshops I have conducted for grieving dads. Watching the barriers come down and the compassion toward each other come out is truly a powerful sight. Many of the dads walk out of these workshops with a lighter load, having learned that it's okay to cry around another guy or to reach out and give another hurting dad a hug.

I have to admit, it's a little weird at first. After all, guys aren't real big on hugging other guys. But once you get past that, the connection becomes obvious — and after that, a true brotherhood starts to form. It doesn't happen overnight, but with a little bit of patience and a lot of commitment, it happens eventually.

In this chapter, we met three dads who offer us the long view on grief, along with what it's taken to sustain them through the years. As I see it, the accounts of their experiences demonstrate how life does indeed go on — even after the worst that life and death can possibly throw our way. Though life goes on, one has to accept that it will look nothing like it was prior to the loss. That's not necessarily a bad thing, but it takes time to get comfortable with the new you.

It's not easy to accept that we are different — very different — after we have laid our children to rest. But different is sometimes good; I have met hundreds of dads who have gone on to accomplish unbelievable things as a way to honor their child. The point is, when the fog starts to lift, there will be a sense of clarity and the desire (and the internal need) to help others or create a legacy for your children. I ask you not to ignore or dismiss those thoughts. Find a way to embrace them instead. It may take some time, but hang on to them as a way of providing a sense of hope. I do believe it is our children's way of offering us a new purpose in life.

One of the most important things Jon, Tony, and Joe can teach us is that helping others is a lifeline of hope and healing. Their stories are, to me, living testaments for every grieving dad that there is reason to continue living — and that it's even possible to have a rewarding, fulfilling life after the death of a child.

CHAPTER 9

UNEXPECTED POSITIVES

ALREADY I KNOW what you are thinking, and you are right.

You are thinking there is *nothing* positive about the death of a child. And as I just said, you are right. There is simply nothing on this earth that could possibly be worse than the passing of a child. Remember the words of Phil, back in chapter two? He said, "There isn't anything worse than the loss of a child, and if there is, I don't want to know about it."

He's right, too.

But whether you are willing to believe what I'm going to say next or not, I promise you that every grieving dad can turn this most negative thing imaginable into something that's completely unexpected.

Something positive, to be specific.

How? How is such a thing possible in the face of such inconceivably crushing circumstances? Well, I submit to you it's not only *possible,* but it's actually quite a bit more common than you would ever think. After the death of a child, the creation of something positive happens *frequently,* believe it or not. It happens because grieving dads who are going through the worst experiences of their lives sometimes also go through significant transformations. Ones that never would have happened otherwise.

Now is a good time to clarify what I'm saying. I am not suggesting that any grieving dad (given the choice) would ever trade "unexpected positives" for the child they lost to death. I know I wouldn't. And I can confidently speak on behalf of the fathers I've interviewed when I say they wouldn't, either. But nevertheless, I'll say it once more:

After the death of a child, the creation
of something positive is a frequent occurrence.

Now is a good time to think about that for a second. If what I'm saying sounds preposterous, take a moment to reflect upon some of the things that have happened in human history — things that happened as a result (direct or indirect) of the passing of a child:

— The Economic Research Institute estimates there are over 1.4 million (non-religious) charitable organizations in the U.S. Many thousands of those began as memorial foundations or grief services organizations that help millions of people deal with the death of a loved one. It is impossible to pinpoint how many were directly related to child loss, but you get the point.

— For many years, scholars have speculated that after the death of his only son, William Shakespeare's work was influenced in positive ways. Connections between his son's passing and Shakespeare works such as *Hamlet, Romeo and Juliet, Julius Caesar,* and *Twelfth Night* have been cited as examples.

— President Abraham Lincoln, whose son, William, died in 1862, was described by aides, White House staffers, and those who knew him well, as markedly different after the boy's passing. One such person commented, "Ever after there was a new quality about his demeanor — something approaching awe." Indeed, "awe" seems to be a word that is most appropriate for the way Americans remember Abraham Lincoln today.

— Charles Darwin, the 19th century naturalist who is responsible for the theory of evolution, experienced the death of his 10-year-old daughter,

Annie, in 1851. Much later, in a 2002 book published by his great-great-grandson, it came out that Darwin's work was influenced by Annie's passing. Regardless of your stance on the science versus divine intervention debate, most would agree that Darwin's theories are as important to mankind as those presented by the likes of Albert Einstein and Isaac Newton.

— In 1991, Eric Clapton, the famed rock and blues artist, wrote *Tears in Heaven* to honor the passing of his son, Connor. The popular tune would become Song of the Year at the 1993 Grammy Awards, and it has touched the lives of millions of people, reminding all of us how fragile and precious young life truly is.

— The 1993 kidnapping and murder of Polly Klaas made international news, and is partially credited with the formation of the "three strikes" law in California and other states. In the wake of his daughter's death, Marc Klaas started Beyond Missing, an organization dedicated to assisting law enforcement with finding missing children. According to the Beyond Missing website, registered users have recovered nearly 300 children since the not-for-profit firm's inception in 2002.

I could go on and on. But how about we turn our attention back to this book? Of course, the whole concept of providing a resource directed exclusively toward grieving dads is a direct result of the fact that I lost my two children. This book has given me purpose, and along with that, has become a powerful reason for living. Not just "living" in the survival sense (not that there isn't value in surviving, mind you) but living in a very meaningful sense.

As in really *living.*

Other grieving dads I've interviewed agree on the subject of unexpected positives. We're going to have a look at two of them, beginning with Craig.

My first encounter with Craig happened because of this book, when I received a survey response from him. The one thing that really caught my eye about his survey was his response to the question: "How has the loss of your child impacted your life?" Craig's reply was, "Transformative (positive) to the point of considering major career change."

Did you happen to catch his use of the word, "positive"?

107

Well, I did. And after reading about how his only child, Abby, had died — and just as importantly, how he has responded since — I had strong hopes that Craig would agree to an interview. Fortunately, he did.

Craig's daughter was only 10 years old when she passed away. Her passing was most unwelcome, but it was not entirely unexpected. In addition to being born with Down's syndrome, the little girl had an advanced case of leukemia. Like many children who carry the disease, she would eventually die more as a result of the treatment than of the affliction itself. In Abby's situation, the aggressive chemotherapy that was employed caused congestive heart failure, which took her life in October, 2008.

Despite the continued insistence by her doctors that Abby's condition would inevitably take her life, for many years Craig didn't want to accept that it was going to happen. In our interview, he told me that his wife had started the grieving process about a year before Abby died. In a way, he was envious of that, and he pointed to the differences in the way men and women grieve as we talked.

"She knew that Abby would eventually die — her condition would be such that she would pass — it was only a matter of time," he said. "Me, on the other hand — not like I was ignorant, but I kept my head in the sand. Mostly, I kept a real positive attitude that it was never going to happen. I never said as much outwardly but in my head, [I thought] 'Let's just keep it positive, let's keep this going for as long as we can.' Then, when it finally happened, it was like 'Whoa!' for me, and for my wife, she had already been grieving and it wasn't as much of a traumatic shock to her."

Craig says that his wife loved their daughter every bit as much as he did, but she responded to Abby's death in a whole different way. "For her, it wasn't like 'Oh my gosh my life is over,' it was more like, 'Well, we're here now and I have to continue with my life.' For me it was like, 'Wait a minute, what just happened?' It was all of a sudden, bam, now she's dead — what do I do?"

According to Craig, many of the professionals he's spoken with say the most important thing married couples can do when they lose a child is to allow each other that space to grieve the way they need to grieve. "There's certain days that I'm going to feel really sad and certain days that she does," Craig told me. "She can think, 'Well, how come you're not crying? Why aren't you sad?' [To me] that's not what's up today for that person. I've learned a lot about myself and my wife as well."

During the family's journey through Abby's challenges with her disease, Craig felt very supported. He was hired as a church office administrator shortly after his daughter's heart condition was diagnosed, and he is still grateful for the flexibility he was given while he worked there. He made it to all of Abby's medical appointments, and when the couple made the choice to set up hospice for their daughter, Craig went on leave for the better part of a month and a half. "There was no pressure," he said, "and for the last part of her life I didn't have to work, and I was paid for it." Many of the people Craig met through the church where he worked didn't quite know what to say to him after Abby passed. Sounds like another constant, right? Again, if a person hasn't experienced the death of their own child, they can't be expected to understand what it's like. They are not in any position to understand what someone who has lost a child is going through. "They don't know how to navigate it," Craig says. "The average church member doesn't quite know what to say or do. You would think in a Christian-based organization that they might know. I've come to realize that it has nothing to do with religion but has everything to do with just experiencing loss. If you haven't, it's really hard to reach out to someone and figure out how to help them."

Still, Craig and his wife felt the community at the church supported them well. In addition to allowing Craig to stay on as an employee, church members kept the family fed for the better part of two months after Abby died. "We had meals every night for a couple of months," Craig told me.

Craig comes from a solid family background. He was raised in New England as a Catholic, and there was a great support system from his family over the years. Coming from a conservative household, his first career decision was to attend the United States Military Academy, and he spent about six years in active duty for the Army. He believes his training in the military taught him to "keep a strong upper lip and drive on."

"When Abby passed, I decided to turn myself in, whatever that means. My wife dealt with her grief a completely different way than I did. The group thing just wasn't for her, but we decided early on to allow ourselves to grieve as we needed. For me, it was going to this group and getting group help and developing friendships that I still have now with these folks. I can pick up the phone any moment and have a conversation and they know exactly where I'm coming from," Craig related.

I asked Craig how well the group therapy worked for him. "I think for me, that was the thing I needed to do," he said. "Otherwise, I would have just sort of soldiered on with my life with this huge cloud over my head."

Craig's experience with bereavement groups evolved over time. For about nine months, he attended a group geared toward couples, then discovered an alternate group that was aimed exclusively at men.

"They ask you to do one or the other," Craig explained. "In this group there were only men who lost children, some wives, brothers, or sisters. There was one man who had lost his [male] partner. That was really incredible; I didn't look at anybody in that group other than as having lost someone they loved."

When I asked Craig how that affected him, he said, "I've changed my outlook on life in general, how I look at things and stereotypes I might have. When someone experiences a loss, it doesn't matter if it is a husband, wife, partner, dog, cat, whatever — it really rips their insides out. When you experience your own loss, you can't help but want to help that person."

Because of that, Craig told me, the friendships he developed in these groups (particularly the all-men's group) feel deeper and more real than his everyday friendships. "There's this element of connection," Craig continued. "You can sit in a room with a guy who's lost a child and you don't have to say anything and a thousand words have been expressed."

One grieving dad Craig met in his church group lost a son to a heart condition. Craig knew the man through church before either of them experienced the death of their children, but they weren't exactly what you would call close. "But since Abby passed, we've become closer and gotten things done together. Now we see each other at church, and when we ask each other how we are doing, it means something different than when we ask our other friends. It's an interesting concept."

Yes it is, Craig.

The transformation in Craig's life since Abby died is even more interesting. So are his views about the big picture of going through his daughter's death.

"Even in looking at the whole thing," Craig conveyed, "as weird as it may sound, experiencing her death was a very mystical, rewarding experience. I brought this child into life and I saw her take her last breath when she left this life. You typically don't get to experience that — as a child, you're supposed to bury your parent — not the other way around."

I must admit, this way of thinking was new to me, so I asked Craig for some clarification.

"It took me a while, but there is something amazing about this whole thing. It's not that I *wanted* it. There's no other way to explain it, except that not many people experience this whole life/death thing with your child. It's transformed me. As incredibly painful as it's been, that night watching her take her last breath, brings me to tears sometimes but then I think that [it] was a privilege."

Let me tell you, Craig's unique perspective about Abby's passing got my attention for sure. I hope it's already gotten yours, but just in case, consider these final words from my interview with Craig:

"I don't want to make it like I'm living out her desires. It's more like, 'What can I do to help other people?' That's why I'm considering going back to school to be a social worker. It will allow me to do something that I know was precipitated by the death of my daughter. It's almost as if her death has freed me up to be who I was really supposed to be."

Partly because of profound thoughts like those, I feel a unique connection to Craig. Many of the things I heard — and ultimately, *learned* from Craig — have resonated with me in a very big way. I am grateful to Craig for that, and I hope Craig's reflections help you to see a few unexpected positives of your own — just as they did for me. And as Craig shared with me, it is truly *my unfortunate honor* to have met not only Craig, but all of the grieving dads and moms that reached out to me during the development of this book.

--

Earlier in this chapter, I mentioned there were two grieving dads that come to mind when the subject of unexpected positives is considered. We'll introduce the second one now. His name is Joe.

Joe's 20-year-old son, Christopher, died back in 2002, the victim of a car accident in which his mother was seriously injured. To this day, Joe has not had the desire to digest the medical records that might point to the precise cause of Christopher's death, but speculation includes head and neck trauma due to the vehicle flipping onto its roof and rolling over up to seven times. Christopher was a tall guy, standing at six foot eight inches — so it's likely that his height was a major disadvantage to him during the accident.

About a year before the accident, Joe's son had undergone an operation to repair a hole in his heart, which was a birth defect. During the operation, the doctors discovered Christopher's heart was also enlarged, so between the planned surgery and the unplanned discovery, Christopher was laid up for quite a while after the operation. By the time he felt ready to go back to college, it was fall of the following year (2002). Even though Christopher had progressed to the point that he was taking classes again, he wasn't exempt from episodes of pain or cautious advice from doctors to avoid "overdoing" things.

Right around Christmas Eve in 2002, Joe's wife and younger son decided to make the 7-hour drive to Christopher's grandparents' home in North Carolina. Christopher had promised his mother he'd go as well, but the night before the scheduled departure, he developed a strange migraine headache. He asked Joe for some Tylenol. "He had played basketball earlier with his friends and I hoped he hadn't overdone it," Joe said. "So I gave him the Tylenol and I told him that if he was still having headaches the next morning, I would have him stay home and I would take him to the doctor."

When Christopher woke up the next morning, his headache was still there but had subsided to a reasonable level. Joe didn't press the point, and both of his sons left with their mother for North Carolina at around 9:00 a.m. Joe stayed behind.

"I was at home in the afternoon and then I got this call from an assistant person at the hospital," Joe continued. "She said, 'I would like to inform you that your family was involved in a car accident. Your wife is in surgery. Your youngest son is doing okay. He wasn't hurt.' But she wouldn't tell me anything about my older son."

When Joe pressed her for details about Christopher, the hospital staffer asked, "Will someone be coming with you?" At that moment, Joe knew something was terribly wrong. Shortly thereafter, a church elder that Joe called showed up in his driveway, with the elder's wife and Joe's best friend in tow. "When I saw them drive up, I knew Christopher didn't make it." The hospital had informed the elder of that very fact, confirming Joe's worst fears.

The church elder and Joe's friend drove him to the hospital where Joe's family was admitted, and the one thing Joe remembers about the long drive was telling his buddy that if Christopher was gone, it was because God had decided it was Christopher's time.

Joe told me that his strong Christian faith has sustained him through the ordeal that ensued. In the wake of the accident, he was facing not only the death of his oldest son, but also a long hospital stay for his wife. In fact, Joe's wife was hospitalized during their son's funeral and thus she couldn't attend. There would also be two months of physical therapy for her when she was finally released, three months after the accident occurred.

Both Joe and his wife had to deal with guilt, each for different reasons.

Joe's guilt stemmed from the fact he didn't insist that Christopher stay behind, which would have allowed his son to avoid the accident in the first place. "That haunted me for a long time but afterwards, I started reading all kinds of books," Joe says. "I plunged myself into reading all I could about grief. All of a sudden, the window opened up to show there was a lot of hurting people out there. People I didn't see before."

He went on to draw an analogy that hit home with me. "It's like when I decide I'm going to buy a new car, I notice that car everywhere. It's not like I've been looking for it, but because I've decided on it, my instinct and senses are keying in on that car and I recognize it. It was the same way with grief and losing a child and all of a sudden, I see people out here hurting, walking down the street and right next door."

The opening of this window has meant that Joe is now more sensitive to people and their grieving process. It also led to Joe making the decision to join the Worldwide Discipleship Association (WDA), which operates a restorative ministry to help people. In the group meetings sponsored by the association, "the women lead the women, and the guys lead the guys," Joe says. "We found that if they are together, especially a husband and a wife in the same group, the husband will focus on the wife and never focus on his own issues."

Joe believes that this gender-driven approach to group counseling helps the men to discover what is causing their own pain, which ultimately helps them to deal with it and support each other in a nonjudgmental environment. And in the aftermath of Christopher's death, Joe has found his work with WDA to be an unexpected positive in its own right.

"The group is a commitment for 17 weeks, 17 lessons that we go through," Joe explained. "We go through and we let them know that this is a support group to either teach you how to be a safe person or how to look for a safe person [to confide in]. The ministry we do — the book is written for anybody, it's not religious-affiliated."

I asked Joe if his work with the WDA was akin to connecting grieving fathers with other grieving fathers. He replied, "That's what we are doing, and they see the value of this, going outside of the church. I also see this as one-on-one, meeting with dads to help them through this. That's what we do with this 17-week program. We train people to do this so that when we leave, they can pick up the ball and start training others."

That philosophy has fed on itself effectively, to the point where social and clinical organizations needing professional counselors on staff have turned to Joe and his colleagues for help. "We go in and train them. We want to train them to [operate] a group."

Reaching out to others, and *using* the strong emotions related to the death of a child in a way that helps other grieving dads, has become another notch in the unexpected positives belt for Joe. The same is true for many other grieving dads I've interviewed, some of whom will say that without their strong commitment to helping others, their lives would carry far less meaning.

I certainly know that to be true in my own case.

Today, Joe finds additional meaning in advising newly bereaved fathers, and helping them find ways to survive the death of their children. First, he suggests that whatever you're going through, it's normal. Secondly, he says that grieving dads need to get involved with a support group. "You need to have another male or a group of males outside of the family system," he says. "The males understand the male side of it. The males need to really try and bond. What you're going through right now is normal, and everyone who has lost a child goes through these stages, these waves, at some point in their lives."

It's certainly true that a big part of finding the way back from the brink can be established by making a commitment to helping others. In my view, looking at things this way is very much like adopting a "pay it forward" approach, because helping someone else to deal with major adversity can only help you to do the same.

Score another one for unexpected positives. And while we're at it, let's have a look at some of the ones grieving dads have described to me during my interviews:

1. **Loss of the fear of death**: Few things are apt to make a man fear death less than experiencing the death of his child. Many grieving dads reported to me that after their children passed on, fear of death all but disappeared — and in some cases, there is even a sense of anticipation at the thought of seeing their child again in an afterlife scenario.

2. **Greater compassion for others**: Joe's recollections about seeing grief everywhere now, when he didn't see it before at all, are a great illustration of this point. Over and over throughout this book, you have seen grieving dads express the sentiment that unless you've been through it, you can't understand what it's like to experience the passing of a child. Fathers such as Joe and Craig from this chapter can show us that harnessing (NOT suppressing) our own emotions and directing them toward others in need can bring a new, optimistic, and rewarding outlook on life.

3. **New and better priorities**: This is another very common theme. Through the development of this book, a significant number of respondents say things that used to be "important" no longer are — and vice versa. In other words, daily pursuit of things like faster cars or nicer golf clubs are usually replaced with renewed commitment to family time or spiritual growth-oriented pastimes. In my own case, I now see beauty in things I never took the time to "take in" before. Going through the death of two children taught me to slow down and spend the time to experience life. Many of the dads I spoke with expressed that walking away from it all, selling everything they own and moving to a place that is less hectic and more peaceful has crossed their mind on more than one occasion.

4. **Greater depth in relationships**: Often, grieving dads experience enhanced intimacy and greater connection with their wives or significant others. The same is true for relationships with surviving children and other members of the grieving dad's community. What's more, many grieving dads point out that new relationships are created through support groups, and lifelong friendships are forged that never would have otherwise begun.

5. **Career changes bringing greater fulfillment**: Take Craig's story from earlier in this chapter to heart. The sense of a higher meaning or a greater purpose in life is often fostered after the death of a child. As a result, many grieving dads consider (and often make) career changes that keep connections to the children that passed on very much alive. Along the way, fathers who take this approach often find the career change itself much more rewarding than whatever they may have been involved with before.

6. **Increased community involvement**: Stories like the ones Craig and Joe told here in this very chapter are repeated over and over in my interviews with grieving dads. Many worthwhile organizations and community groups were born as a direct result of the passing of a child, and the majority of such groups bring meaningful help and guidance to a wide cross section of needs in communities throughout the world.

7. **Closer relationship with living children**: I touched on this in number four above, but it bears further consideration. Even fathers who haven't experienced the death of a child can benefit from the stories grieving dads have to tell, because there is always an increased awareness of how fragile life really is. Once we understand that concept, our desire to bond with our living children is increased a thousand fold.

There could be many more examples of ways grieving dads can create gain from loss. Sometimes, it's through the adoption of a cause that honors the memory of the children that passed on. Other times, gain is created through becoming a mentor to people in need, or simply by listening to a brother who needs to lighten his load. But always, as is the case with most things in this never-ending mystery we call life, adversity often brings with it the opportunity to enrich the world.

CHAPTER 10

BACK

So HERE WE are, with our little journey to the brink and back nearly complete. We've taken a ride with many of the grieving dads I've interviewed, starting from shock and trauma, stopping for a moment at rock bottom, learning a thing or two about real help, and finally winding up at unexpected positives along the way.

I suspect that at times, you found this book every bit as difficult to read as I did to write it. But if you're like me even a little bit, you also found the trip to be rewarding.

Or better yet, helpful.

You know, so often in my interactions with grieving dads, I've heard the question: "Is this normal?" For a long time after Katie and Noah passed away, I asked myself that question just about every five minutes. I asked my counselor the same thing every time I met with her. True, the context changed all the time, but the common theme of "normal" came up in my head over and over again.

For a few examples, is it normal...

...to lose the fear of dying?

...to feel guilt regarding the death of my child?

...to be pissed at people I don't even know, just because they're laughing at a joke or going on about their life?

...to cry when I hear a song or read a Hallmark card that has nothing to do with my child's passing?

...to experience flashbacks regarding the death of my child?

...to drink until I can't stand up?

...to acquire fears I never had before?

...to punch a wall until I can't feel my hands anymore?

...to utter the words, "fuck you" at the most inappropriate times imaginable?

...to consider killing myself, if only so I could see my child again?

...to feel abandoned by my family and friends?

...to have depression to the point that getting out of bed is a monumental task?

...to feel weak because I need help to survive this pain?

...to be angry at God?

...to physically weep uncontrollably?

...to feel like a different man than I was prior to my child's death?

...to lose interest in sex?

...to lose my job, or worse, not to even care that I lost my job?

...to burst into tears without warning, years after my child passed away?

Please understand that I'm not a doctor, but for once I can tell you there's an answer that works for every one of these questions.

The answer is yes.

"Normal," you see, takes on a whole different meaning for a father who has experienced the death of a child. In fact, the concept of normal goes right out the window when a man is dealing with such extreme circumstances. I'm here to tell you that in my discussions, nearly every grieving dad has experienced at least one of these emotional responses.

At least in that sense, I think I've proven my point. If you don't think so, that's okay. It probably means you're reading this book from a very different perspective — most likely, the one that comes from not having experienced the death of a child.

For those of us who have, notions of "normal" and certainly, of a "normal life," died with the passing of our children. Mind you, that doesn't mean *life* died when our children did. It just means the life we once knew has changed forever.

But changed or not, I promise you that life for a grieving dad doesn't have to be reduced to (or defined by) little more than despair during every waking hour. And with that in mind, I thought I would share a few more insights from the grieving dads I've encountered during the time I've been engaged with the development of this book.

Here are a few thought-provoking quotes for you to ponder:

"Society doesn't know what to say: 'He's in a better place, God must have needed another angel, things will work out.' That's the last thing someone wants to hear. I could have given a rip that God needed my son. We wanted him." – Phil, OR

"Pray for strength, pray for help, and ask your child to come to you. Speak to your child like they are with you, because I believe they are." – Bob, GA

"This journey takes more time than what people who are looking in from the outside might expect. Not 2-3 years but 7-10." – Kent, Canada

"Most friends or family you don't want to lose contact with, you will have to reach out to. Except for a few people, most don't 'get it' and never will. Some will

not be responsive and you will just have to resign yourself that they can't handle it." – Matt, NY

"There are more of us out there than you think — many people you pass on the street have gone through the same thing. This is a bad club to be a part of, but most members are willing to help because they get it. Everything is right — all of the emotions are okay. For you it is right. Let the journey happen." – Angelo, IL

"Crying cleanses the soul. Power can come from crying. To assume that tears are a sign of weakness is to miss the truth about life." – Charlie, NY

"You have to talk about it and let it out. Cry a lot. Remember the good times with your child. Celebrate your child's life. Try to help a lot of people." – Don, NM

"I would tell another bereaved father that I am truly sorry for their loss and I would ask them their child's name. I would tell them to let all the emotions out and not to let people put expectations on them and their grieving process. I would tell them everybody grieves differently. I would tell them to ignore people who haven't lost a child, especially those trying to equate it to losing a parent or grandparent. I would tell them it's a long journey that will take them through the rest of their life. I'd tell them the pain does get less acute but never goes away." – Steve, MA

"The most important thing is to take it one day, one minute, at a time. No matter how difficult it may be at this time, it will get better, slowly, but it will get better. No one grieves the same and there is no timetable for grief." – Gary, ME

"There is hope…and there are more of us out there when you need us." – Leonard, TX

"Time will help a lot. Allow yourself to grieve in the way that works for you — if you feel the need to visit the cemetery everyday for the first year, then do it. Find something positive to do in memory of your child. Allow the tragedy to motivate you to live a better life." – Dave, MS

"Talk about it. Share your stories, don't let others tell you how to grieve or how long to grieve. Do what you feel is right. Tell people when they say something

offensive — don't hold it in. Cry as often as you need to. I'm a cop (30 year vet) and crying isn't something we do…well I do now and I am proud of it." – Mitch, CA

"Get counseling ASAP, do not wait — even if you think you are okay. I found the first year I was in a state of numbness, followed by a complete collapse of emotions." – Cory, MA

"Hang-on — it is going to be a bumpy road. Use any and all tools available to help you get through the pain." – Jeff, CO

"The death of my daughter has brought eternal perspective into every aspect of my life and enabled me to help others in their grief." – Greg, NY

"I have lived two lives, before his death and after. For the longest time, I felt terrible about feeling normal. The first time I laughed, I cried. Why am I feeling happy? But it's one hill at a time, you just climb over it. There's no playbook, no instruction manual." – Joe, NY

"Be prepared to experience the full cycle of emotions and most importantly, allow yourself to experience those emotions." – Hank, AZ

"Don't wait for normalcy to return — it won't. Give yourself time to deal with the loss and do it in your own way. Don't let anyone tell you how to feel or that it has been long enough."
– Sheldon, VA

"I am more forgiving and less judgmental toward most people, realizing that I have no idea what personal tragedy they may be dealing with. I am trying to be a better person and allowing my son to live through me. Few things in life have any true meaning for me anymore. At the end of the day, most everything seems completely insignificant." – Jeff, MO

"I'm not the rock I used to be. I'm not embarrassed to be seen emotionally upset. That's good, since I don't have much choice." – Ernie, KY

"Your sadness will not go away, but you will live again, which is exactly what your child would want for you." – Matt, MA

This last one has always stuck with me. And it's helped to keep me on mission, reminding me of the very things I was looking for when I was a newly bereaved father. Lest you forget, there simply isn't nearly as much in the way of resources for grieving dads as there is for grieving moms.

That's one of the major reasons why I wrote this book. Another reason is that I wanted to raise awareness about the experiences of a grieving dad — not only for myself, not only for other grieving dads, but really for anyone who has ever loved a child.

Finally, I wrote this book because of hope. Hope that through the telling of these stories and the lessons they carry, grieving dads all over the world will come to understand there is value and meaning in this new existence. For many of us, that means being there for those who still love and need us — and drawing strength simply from *being* loved and needed. For others, it means understanding we still have much to offer to this world, even if our children aren't here to see us deliver.

Of course, most of us believe they're watching anyway.

Yes, this is the book I never wanted to write. But now that I have, there is a new sense of anticipation I never thought I'd feel after Katie and Noah died. It's the sense that if our children are indeed watching us, they would have a thing or two to tell us.

They would tell us it's okay to miss them.

They would tell us it's okay to cry.

They would tell us it's okay to worry, to remember, to be angry, to love, and to laugh.

But above all, they would tell us that it's okay to live.

ACKNOWLEDGMENTS

I am truly honored and will be forever grateful for the trust that all the grieving dads have given me throughout this project. These men trusted me enough to share not only their stories, but also to allow me a brief glance at the pain and suffering they carry around with them as a result of their losses.

These men were kind enough to relive some of those very dark days, and gracious enough to share their stories so other men can gain insight about the impacts the death of a child can have on one's life.

These men knew their stories would be shared in this book. However, they still wanted to be a part of something that reaches out to other grieving dads, hopefully in a way that helps them to understand they are not alone in this journey. Further, the grieving dads I interviewed for this book all wanted to make it clear that they truly care about the survival of grieving dads all over the world — and more than that, they care about victory, over the darkest, most crushing kind of loss a human being could possibly ever experience.

Although the stories of these grieving dads are heartfelt and honest, many of the names in this book have been changed to protect the privacy of the men I interviewed.

ABOUT KELLY FARLEY

KELLY FARLEY, like many men, was caught up in the rat race of life when he experienced the loss of two babies over an 18-month period. *He lost his daughter, Katie, in 2004, and son, Noah, in 2006.* During the losses and the years that followed, he felt like he was the only dad that had ever experienced such a loss. He realized that society, for the most part, doesn't feel comfortable with an openly grieving male. That realization inspired him to write this book.

In addition to this book, Kelly maintains a blog at GrievingDads.com and is currently pursuing his M.S. Ed. degree in counseling to continue his mission of helping others through profound life experiences.

Kelly was raised in Iowa and currently lives in the suburbs of Chicago. He enjoys spending time with his wife, Christine, and his dog, Buddy.

COACHING AND SPEAKING

Kelly Farley has a passion for helping people "pick up the pieces" after a profound life event. He is available to work with you as your personal coach to help you put your life back together. Kelly is also available to speak at your event or conduct his training seminars. If you are interested in working with Kelly, please contact him:

Grieving Dads LLC
Kelly@GrievingDads.com
(630) 561-5989
Or visit his website at www.GrievingDads.com